Classical Athens

THE BRITISH MUSEUM PRESS

Acknowledgements

Many friends and colleagues have generously given their time, encouragement and expertise during the writing of this book; it is due to their support that the book has come to fruition in the face of difficult circumstances. Grateful thanks are due in particular to Judith Binder, Susan Deacy, Susanne Ebbinghaus, Maria Effinger, Lesley Fitton, Bethan Hobbs, Karin Hornig, Ian Jenkins, Astrid Lindenlauf, Nino Luraghi, Emma McAllister, Astrid Möller, Jenny Newell, Thorsten Opper, Katerina Panagopoulou, Stavros Paspalas, Valerie Smallwood, Judith Swaddling, Frank Wascheck, Dyfri Williams, Richard Woff, and Susan Woodford. David Cahn, Dudley Hubbard, Mario Iozzo, Michael Krumme, and Doris Vollkommer kindly assisted in sourcing photographs, and Kate Morton expertly designed a new map of Classical Athens. At BMP, Nina Shandloff, Beatriz Waters and in particular Charlie Mounter and Isabel Andrews, with unfailing encouragement and patience, saw the book through to publication. All remaining errors are, of course, my own.

The book is dedicated to my parents and to my friends, who have once more proven Menander right: Οὐκ ἔστιν οὐδὲν κτῆμα κάλλιον φίλου – There is no possession lovelier than a friend.

First published in 2005 by The British Museum Press
A division of The British Museum Company Ltd
38 Russell Square
London WC1B 3QQ

Alexandra Villing has asserted the right to be identified as author
of this work

A catalogue record for this book is available from the British Library

ISBN 0 7141 2792 2
ISBN 9 780714 127927

Designed and typeset in Galliard by Andrew Shoolbred

Printed and bound in China by C&C Offset Printing Co., Ltd

Contents

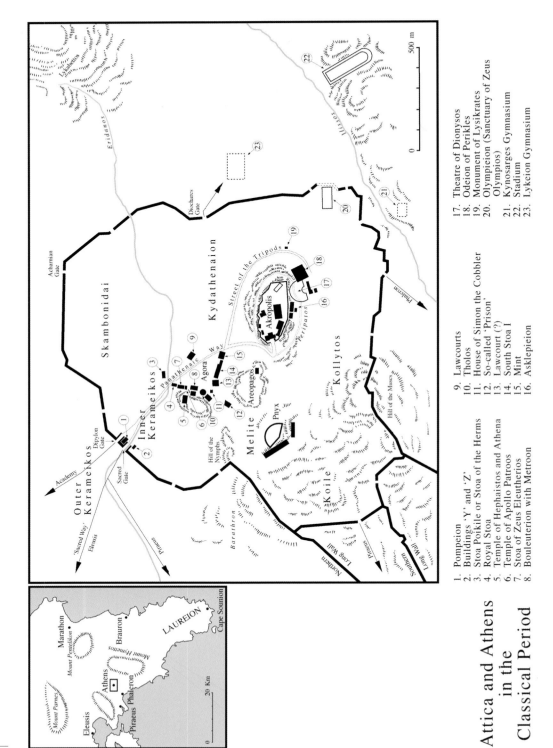

Attica and Athens in the Classical Period

1. Pompeion
2. Buildings 'Y' and 'Z'
3. Stoa Poikile or Stoa of the Herms
4. Royal Stoa
5. Temple of Hephaistos and Athena
6. Temple of Apollo Patroos
7. Stoa of Zeus Eleutherios
8. Bouleuterion with Metroon
9. Lawcourts
10. Tholos
11. House of Simon the Cobbler
12. So-called 'Prison'
13. Lawcourt (?)
14. South Stoa I
15. Mint
16. Asklepieion
17. Theatre of Dionysos
18. Odeion of Perikles
19. Monument of Lysikrates
20. Olympieion (Sanctuary of Zeus Olympios)
21. Kynosarges Gymnasium
22. Stadium
23. Lykeion Gymnasium

Mistress of the world, august city of Athens,
how perfectly beautiful appears your arsenal,
how beautiful the Parthenon, and how beautiful the Piraeus!
What other city ever had such parks?
It stands, as they say, in the beauty of heaven.
(Anonymous Comic poet, fr. 155 K.-A.)

Athens from the south west in about 1805/6. Watercolour by Sir William Gell (1777–1836)

The Panathenaic procession winds its way up the Akropolis, towards the burning altar of Athena. In the foreground the Propylaia with the temple of Athena Nike to the right of the approach ramp. The statue of Athena Promachos and the Erechtheion are straight ahead, the Parthenon is to the right, with the precinct of Artemis Brauronia in front. The ceremonial Panathenaic ship is lower down the slope outside the gates on the left, next to the Klepsydra fountain house.

View of the Akropolis from below the Hephaisteion looking across the Agora. Remains of the Bouleuterion and Metroon and the stone fence of the Monument of the Eponymous Heroes are in the foreground, columns belonging to the South Stoa are visible on the right and the edge of the Stoa of Attalos on the very left. On the Akropolis, the Athena Nike Temple has been removed from the bastion jutting out to the right for restoration (2003).

ABOVE
An Athenian wedding procession: a chariot takes bride and bridegroom from the house of the bride's father to the bridegroom's house, accompanied by torchbearers and women carrying gifts. Attic red-figure *pyxis* (box), about 430 BC.

LEFT
A seated woman reading from a book-scroll and three companions. An unusual scene, as women in Classical Athens were not normally able to read. Attic red-figure *hydria* (water-jar), about 450 BC.

LEFT
Two Athenian boys playing with toy carts, jugs and grapes. Attic red-figure *chous* (jug), about 420–410 BC.

RIGHT
Thanatos (Death) and Hypnos (Sleep) carry the body of a warrior to his tomb. Attic white-ground *lekythos* (oil flask), about 430 BC.

The cast of a satyr play in the sanctuary of Dionysos, gathered around the piper Pronomos and the playwright Demetrios, whose names are inscribed on the vase. Attic red-figure volute-*krater* (wine bowl), about 400 BC.

Chariot race at the Panathenaic Games: a four-horse chariot rounding the post. Attic black-figure Panathenaic Prize *amphora* (olive oil jar), about 420–400 BC.

Introduction: Building a myth

When in 79 BC the Roman statesman and philosopher Cicero and his friends set out on a walk from the Dipylon gate in the walls of Athens to Plato's Academy, they are struck by the power of places to evoke history, and to evoke the people who shaped this history some five hundred years before their time. The Academy calls up thoughts of the philosopher Plato; the village of Kolonos conjures up images of the playwright Sophokles and of the hero Oedipus; the bay of Phaleron evokes the orator Demosthenes declaiming on the beach 'to learn to pitch his voice so as to overcome an uproar'. As Lucius, Cicero's cousin, exclaims, 'there is no end to it in this city; wherever you go you tread historic ground.'

Athens is indeed a city full of memories of times past, and particularly of its greatest glory in the Classical period. How Athens was laid out at this time becomes clear from a glance at the map (left): the city encloses the Akropolis like a pearl in an oyster. The 'high city' itself is surrounded by two important 'ring roads', the Peripatos hugging the lower slopes of the Akropolis, and the busier Street of the Tripods further out. On the south side these thoroughfares linked the theatre of Dionysos with other festival buildings; on the north they led to the Agora, the commercial heart of the city and the seat of many democratic institutions. Framing the Agora to the west is a low hill, the Kolonos Agoraios, topped by the temple of Hephaistos and Athena, while to the south is the Areopagos, the Hill of Ares, where the council of elders met before the fall of the tyranny at the end of the sixth century BC. This arc is echoed further to the south-west by a range of low hills near the middle of which is located the Pnyx, the home of the democratic assembly in the fifth and fourth centuries BC. Beyond, on all sides, lay the people's city, essentially residential, perhaps the flesh of the oyster, divided up into the demes, or boroughs, of Skambonidai, Kydathenaion, Kollytos, Koile, and Melite. The oyster's shell, of course, was formed by the city walls, hastily erected after the defeat of the Persians, but later reinforced and rebuilt, and punctuated in more than a dozen places by gates that issued on to the roads radiating from the city to its life-giving countryside.

Outside the walls themselves were the cemeteries, for it was customary in Greece to bury the dead only beyond the city walls, together with workshops too large to fit within the city's confines. Beyond them, in the open 'greenfield' zone, were to spring up the gymnasia or training grounds, where youths prepared for manhood and men prepared for war. To the southwest, at the other end of the dumb-bells formed by the Long Walls, lay the Piraeus with its three harbours, a city in its own right but also the mouth for the hungry mother city, the gateway for trade with all the known world across the Mediterranean and beyond.

Most of the buildings and monuments of this, the Classical city, have long been lost to the ravages of time and the ancient city's layout has become obscured by the sprawl of modern developments. But even if no longer a visible, living city, Classical Athens is still much alive in our minds. We are surrounded by elements of Classical Athenian architecture, can still see Athenian tragedies being staged, read Athenian philosophy, and we remain attracted by Athenian ideas of aesthetic beauty, harmony, and rational reasoning. The world of Perikles and Pheidias, of Sophokles and Plato seems close to our own. On closer inspection, however, Classical Athens also reveals itself as a foreign world in which much would seem rather less than ideal. It was a place of comparatively little privacy, of relative poverty, a society based on slavery and gender segregation where democracy was restricted to male full citizens only, a world of coarse jokes that would cause storms of outrage and litigation were they broadcast on television today, a world in which prostitution was socially acceptable and homosexual relationships between older men and boys were considered educational.

These ideas and beliefs, be they familiar or foreign to us today, are what shaped the lives of the ancient Athenians as they attended the assembly or the theatre, gossiped in the market, worshipped their gods, and went about their daily lives in the two centuries that make up what we now call the Classical period. These were turbulent and fast-moving times that had seen Athens rise from being just one of hundreds of independent city states to become the main power in Greece in the fifth century BC, as well as the first democratic state in world history. Crucial in this rise was the decisive role that Athens had played in the defeat of the Persians, who attacked Greece in the early fifth century BC and were beaten back against all odds by a joint Greek effort under the leadership of Athens and Sparta. This experience accelerated the development of Athenian democracy, which had replaced tyranny already in the late sixth century BC. With democracy the arts, notably architecture, sculpture, theatre, and philosophy, prospered too. Yet by the second half of the fifth century BC, Athens' domination of other Greek city states had taken on the shape of a repressive empire. In the subsequent war against its rival, Sparta, a war that lasted (with interruptions) for nearly thirty years, it irrevocably lost its position of power. The memory of the glory of its heyday, however, lived on, especially as the Athenians themselves began in the fourth century BC to reflect on their achievements.

As a result of this lasting historical significance, Athens has continued to attract visitors who want to breathe the spirit of the place. The first true tourists were perhaps Greeks from Asia Minor in the Roman period, for whom Pausanias in the second century AD wrote his 'Guide to Greece', the first travel guidebook.

For a long time thereafter, however, the Western world had only a nebulous idea of the city of Athens. Few travellers from Western Europe ever reached this destination, at first part of the Byzantine Empire, then under Frankish rule. Among those who did visit Athens was Cyriacus of Ancona, who, in 1447, lamented that the city was just a heap of ruins. Soon after, Athens fell to the Turks, and prospered moderately under Ottoman rule.

With the Age of Enlightenment and the appeal exerted by ancient Greek philosophy and politics on eighteenth century Western thinking, Athens was rediscovered as the cradle of the ideal of democracy and the free human spirit, initiating a flow of visitors that continues to this day. What an eighteenth century visitor encountered would have been very different from the sprawling, bustling modern city of today. Athens in those days was a small, picturesque town in which the layout of the ancient city with its buildings was still much in evidence. The Englishmen Stuart and Revett were the first to comprehensively document the architectural splendours of these and other Greek buildings to an audience intent on having their own town and country houses built in a Classical Greek style. Perhaps the most famous of Athens' visitors at the time was Lord Elgin, who shook the aesthetic sensibilities of his countrymen when the Parthenon sculptures went on show in London and the reality of Classical Greek sculpture was first appreciated. He was soon followed by Lord Byron, who toured Greece from 1809 and later participated actively in the Greek War of Independence.

Greek independence won, the country's ancient legacy was of paramount importance for the newly founded state, now headed by a Western monarch, King Otto, of the House of Bavaria. Archaeological work began, the main aim being to reveal what was deemed the finest hour of the city of Athens and Greek civilization, the fifth century BC. Later layers (Byzantine, Frankish, Ottoman) were stripped away as archaeologists and politicians, fired by Classicist ideas, sought to return Athens to an ideal Periklean condition. Classical Athens had indeed become 'classical', setting norms and standards for the modern Greek state, as it had for much of Europe before, and to this day it is the Classical period that continues to dominate our picture of ancient Athens.

This book takes the visitor on a walk through the Classical city, pointing out what remains of it amidst the modern buildings and evoking what would once have been there. It starts on the Akropolis with its splendid temples and religious festivals, moving down the Akropolis slopes, past the political meeting places of the democratic assembly, through the bustling market place, through the city's narrow alleyways past houses, shops and sanctuaries, to the city gates and beyond, through the Kerameikos cemetery and the Academy, and finally to the city's harbour, the Piraeus, and out into the Attic countryside, thus exploring not just the major sites and monuments and the role they played in the history of Athens, but also the less prominent aspects that would have been no less significant in the daily life of the Classical Athenian.

1

The Akropolis: citadel and sanctuary

The Akropolis in the history of Athens

The Akropolis with its gleaming marble temples dominates the cityscape of Athens as it has done for thousands of years. A plateau of about five football fields in size, it is by far the most hospitable and yet defensible of the several rocks that stand out from the Athenian plain and was thus the natural choice for early settlers looking for a safe home. It was also a natural place from which to govern, as whoever ruled over the Akropolis ruled over Athens.

The earliest traces of human occupation on the Akropolis date to the Late Neolithic period (c.3000–2800 BC). In the Late Bronze Age, around the fourteenth and thirteenth centuries BC, Mycenaean Greeks developed a fortified citadel similar to the *akropoleis* (high cities) of Mycenae or Tiryns. A circuit wall made of huge blocks of masonry protected the ruler's palace as well as giving shelter to others within its perimeter. These walls were so massive that their remains, still visible just behind the fifth century BC entrance gate, the Propylaia, came to be considered by Classical Athenians as the work of a prehistoric people of far stronger powers. Much of what looks like fortification today is, however, later; an example is the third century AD Beulé gate in front of the Propylaia.

With the collapse of the Mycenaean civilisation Athens, like much of the rest of Greece, succumbed to a sharp fall in living standards during the so-called 'Dark Ages'. The slow recovery from 1100 BC onwards brought with it a change in city life: around the Akropolis, the 'high city', a lower city (*asty*) sprang up, combining houses, business premises, shrines and cemeteries. This city soon developed into the administrative, political, and religious centre of an even larger territory, the Attic countryside. With its farms, ports and natural resources, Attica provided the basis of life for all Athenians. The Akropolis, however, remained the physical and conceptual heart of Athens. Its buildings and their accomplished decoration reflect, like no others, the history of the city from its rise after the Persian Wars to the height of its power in the fifth century BC and its crushing defeat at the hands of its rival Sparta at the end of that century.

The most momentous event in the history of the Akropolis, as of Athens itself, was the Persian invasion. Partly as a result of some Greek mainland cities, including Athens, having assisted the Greek cities of Asia Minor in a revolt against their Persian overlords, Greece had been invaded by a Persian army under their king Dareios in 490 BC but had beaten back the enemy in the battle of Marathon. Although supposedly a mere 192 Athenians died in battle compared to 6,400 Persians, the event had been highly traumatic. The second invasion – of a 100,000-strong army and 600 ships under King Xerxes, son of Dareios, – was no less so. The fall of the brave Spartan contingent that held the pass at Thermopylai resulted in the sack of the Akropolis in 480 BC and the destruction of the lower city of Athens in 479 BC. The ultimate Greek victory, led by Athens, marks the start of the Classical period for Greece, accelerates the development of Athenian democracy, and sees the beginning of nearly a century of Athenian dominance over the Greek world.

A Greek fighting a Persian. The Persian, dressed in a patterned trouser suit and soft skin cap, vainly attempts to defend himself against the naked, heroic Greek warrior. Attic red-figure *oinochoe* (wine jug), about 460 BC.

With power spread out among the whole of the Athenian citizenship and with political (and commercial) life focused on the market place (Agora) in the lower city, the Akropolis now became the preserve of the gods. It was a space for the young democracy to display its piety towards the gods who had granted them phenomenal success. The large dedications of powerful aristocrats that had once dominated the area were now superseded by collective displays of devotion by the whole city. The most impressive of the new offerings were the buildings that were erected from around 448 BC – most notably the Parthenon and the Propylaia – as part of a building programme that had been initiated by Perikles, the leading politician of the time. Often called the 'Periklean building programme', it was, in fact, not just the work of one man but a joint effort by the Athenian state, democratically decreed, publicly financed and supervised by a committee of citizens. Under Perikles, the Athenians set out to rebuild the temples destroyed by the Persians in 480 BC long deliberately left as ruins. From a sad memorial, the Akropolis was transformed into a splendid display of Athenian culture and power, a credit to the gods and the democratic city alike.

Large sculptures or sculptural groups that were dedicated by the state would have crowded around these temples and buildings, next to spoils of war taken from enemies in battle. One such sculpture was the monumental bronze statue of Athena Promachos, the tip of whose spear was said to be visible already to sailors approaching Sounion in southern Attica. Bronze and iron objects, from armour and weapons to metal vessels, were stored in a special building, the Chalkotheke, built in the late fifth or early fourth century BC against the south wall of the Akropolis. But small votive offerings, dedicated by private individuals, would also have filled the space: figurines, bronze objects, stone reliefs and

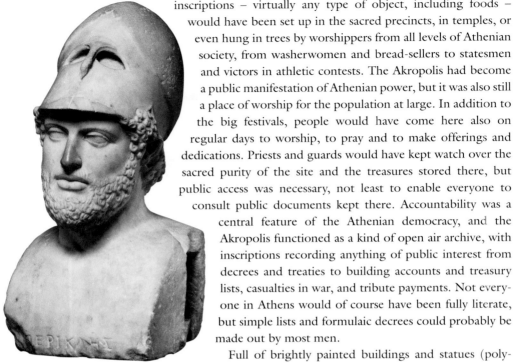

inscriptions – virtually any type of object, including foods – would have been set up in the sacred precincts, in temples, or even hung in trees by worshippers from all levels of Athenian society, from washerwomen and bread-sellers to statesmen and victors in athletic contests. The Akropolis had become a public manifestation of Athenian power, but it was also still a place of worship for the population at large. In addition to the big festivals, people would have come here also on regular days to worship, to pray and to make offerings and dedications. Priests and guards would have kept watch over the sacred purity of the site and the treasures stored there, but public access was necessary, not least to enable everyone to consult public documents kept there. Accountability was a central feature of the Athenian democracy, and the Akropolis functioned as a kind of open air archive, with inscriptions recording anything of public interest from decrees and treaties to building accounts and treasury lists, casualties in war, and tribute payments. Not everyone in Athens would of course have been fully literate, but simple lists and formulaic decrees could probably be made out by most men.

Full of brightly painted buildings and statues (polychromy was a central feature in ancient architecture and sculpture), crowded by inscribed marble slabs recording what was of importance in the city, and overflowing with offerings of all kinds, the Classical Akropolis must have been an infinitely rich and fascinating space quite different from the barren rock with its pristine white ruins of today.

Marble bust of Perikles, Roman, second century AD, after a Greek original of about 430 BC . The helmet alludes to Perikles' position as general, while the even features and calm expression show him to conform to the ideal of an Athenian statesman.

The Akropolis and its cults: Athena and the Panathenaia

Many gods were worshipped in Classical Athens, but none was more at home there than Athena, the Greek goddess of war and wisdom. She was the virgin daughter of Zeus, father of the gods, and was born from his head after he swallowed her pregnant mother, Metis. The early Greek poet Homer reports Athena flying into the house of the mythical Athenian king Erechtheus on the Akropolis, and indeed she may already have been the patron goddess of the Mycenaean rulers residing on the citadel. For Classical Athenians, she was the city goddess, Polias, patroness of all citizens. In addition, she was Parthenos (virgin), Nike (of victory), Hygieia (of health) and Ergane (craftswoman) – a wide range of aspects, each served by its own temple, shrine or at least altar. Her cult was centred, however, on the highly venerated ancient olive wood image of Athena Polias that had supposedly fallen from the sky. It was for Athena Polias that the main Athenian festival, the Panathenaia, was celebrated.

Religious festivals were an essential part of life in Classical Athens, with up to 120 festival days (mostly public) each year. Festivals were vital for the social cohesion of the city. They often incorporated important transition rites for the young, gradually turning them into full members of the community. Some processions linked shrines in the city with shrines in Attica, thus encouraging cohesion between city and countryside. Not least, they were the only opportunity for many Athenians to enjoy the luxury of feasting on roasted meat, while at the same time ensuring the goodwill of the gods.

The most important of these festivals which brought all Athenians together was the Panathenaia. It was held annually at the end of the first Athenian month, Hektatombaion, equivalent to our modern July/early August, the time when, according to myth, Athena had helped the gods defeat the rebellious giants, but also when she had supposedly been born from the head of Zeus. The festival's core was a procession ending in sacrifices on the Akropolis, combined with some competitions, such as a chorus and a dance in armour. From around 566–565 BC it was celebrated every

fourth year in a far more elaborate way: this Great Panathenaia vied with the large ancient panhellenic festivals such as the Olympic games and attracted visitors and participants from all over the Greek world. It lasted for eight days and included musical competitions, recitations of Homer's epic poetry, gymnastic and equestrian contests, such as boxing, wrestling, pentathlon, footraces, horse-races and chariot-races, and events such as dancing in armour, torch races, a male beauty pageant, and a regatta in the harbour. Like virtually anything in democratic Athens, it was, from the late fifth century BC onwards, planned and managed by a board of citizens selected by lot.

Both Athenians and athletes from abroad participated in the Panathenaic games, which essentially occupied the first five days of the festival. Victors stood to win bronze tripods, gold or silver crowns, cash, bulls, but especially large amphorae that depicted both Athena and the relevant competition. These prize-amphorae were filled with the best Athenian olive oil, collected from the sacred groves of Athena. For every Panathenaia at least 1400 amphorae would have been needed, from around 566–565 BC until the second century BC. The finds of these vases all over the Greek world attest both to the wide appeal of the festival itself and to Athenian olive oil as a valued commodity in Mediterranean trade. The prizes were generous: a winner of the *stadion*, a short sprint, in the early fourth century BC received over two thousand litres of oil in sixty such amphorae, which would have provided considerable wealth when sold. But even non-competing participants at the festival were able to take away their souvenirs:

Attic black-figure Panathenaic prize *amphora* (olive oil jar), about 403 BC: The goddess Athena is armed with a shield depicting the statue group of Harmodios and Aristogeiton. They were popularly credited as heroes of the Athenian democracy for having killed the son of the tyrant Peisistratos, Hipparchos, in the late sixth century BC even though their motive was in fact a mere love feud. The rule of the tyrants had until then been quite popular and led to a great economic and cultural flourishing of Athens.

perfumed olive oil called 'Panathenaikon' in miniature replicas of Panathenaic amphorae.

The true religious climax of the festival, however, was the procession that followed the games, winding its way from the edge of town up to the Akropolis. At the Great Panathenaia, both Athenian citizens and non-citizens would have participated, including the athletes, event officials and priests, marshals, musicians, noble youths and maidens, hoplites (warriors on foot) and cavalry. The non-citizen *metoikoi* (metics) carried trays of honey-cakes and their daughters water-jars. Freed slaves and foreigners bearing oak branches are supposed to have joined in too. The procession included some hundred cows, which were to be sacrificed on the great altar of Athena Polias, in front of her temple. There were also smaller sacrifices for Athena Hygieia and Athena Nike. Gifts to the gods were the core of Greek ritual, serving to honour and thank but also to ask for something in return. Animal sacrifices were the most striking of all such gifts. The climax of the Panathenaia, therefore, must have been a particularly bloody spectacle, lasting several hours, accompanied by the ritual screaming of women and bellowing of the animals, as the smoke from the fat being burned as an offering to the goddess darkened the sky. Most of the meat was later distributed to the citizens and a large feast was held where the procession had started. From about 400 BC the nobility dined in a building with a large colonnaded courtyard next to the Dipylon city gate, known as the Pompeion, while the rest of the population feasted in the gate's forecourt and the street beyond.

At the heart of the procession was the special new garment, the *peplos*, for Athena Polias. It had been woven by a small group of girls of noble birth (the Arrhephoroi and the Ergastinai) who had been in the service of Athena over the previous year, and was invariably decorated with the story of the battle between gods and giants. This large square of cloth was attached like a sail to a boat mounted on wheels which was dragged all the way up to the Akropolis gates. The presentation of the *peplos* to the presiding officials forms the centrepiece of the extraordinary frieze that decorates the Parthenon. It was then given to the ancient wooden and, presumably, quite shapeless cult statue of Athena that, from the late fifth century BC, was housed in the Erechtheion.

The Propylaia

Winding its way up to the Akropolis, the Classical Panathenaic procession would have entered the sacred precinct through the Propylaia, an elaborate gateway built under Perikles by the architect Mnesikles between 437 and 432 BC. It replaced a much simpler gate destroyed by the Persians in 480 BC and is still the way by which the modern visitor enters the Akropolis.

The massive gates, the first of their kind and obviously designed to impress, were an architectural masterpiece. They had to accommodate a difficult sloping terrain and give easy access for the large procession as well as achieve a balanced and symmetrical appearance. It is often suspected that the original plan was even larger and more symmetrical, but that disagreements led to last-minute revisions. The façade presents the building as a temple, with six columns of the plain Doric type supporting a gable. Of the two flanking structures, the one on the right is truncated so as to not interfere with the remains of ancient Mycenean walls and the sanctuary of Artemis Brauronia behind it, and gives access to the sanctuary of Athena Nike located on a high spur overlooking the approach (see below). The one on the left leads into a further room. In Roman times this was known as the 'pinakotheke' or 'picture gallery', since pictures were hung in it. Its primary function, however, is more likely to have been a reception and dining room, with couches lining the walls.

The Classical Athenian's first sight upon walking through the Propylaia would have been the colossal bronze statue of a fully armed Athena Promachos (Champion) by Pheidias, erected a few years earlier as a victory monument for the defeat of the Persians with a tenth of the spoils from Marathon. Its appearance is only known from representations on Athenian lamps and coins of the Roman period. Directly behind it lay the ruins of the Old Temple of Athena, destroyed by the Persians. It had been the main focus of cult on the Akropolis and may for some time afterwards have contained a temporary structure to house the ancient cult image of Athena Polias; in the later fifth century BC, the Erechtheion was erected and took over its function. Further to the right lay the Parthenon; although partly obscured by buildings in the sanctuary of Artemis Brauronia, it was in fact carefully aligned with the axis of the Propylaia.

Parthenon East Frieze central scene: the sacred robe of Athena is held up by cult officials in the presence of girls carrying stools and the seated gods Athena and Hephaistos (right) and Hera and Zeus (left). About 438–432 BC.

The Parthenon

The key monument of Classical Athens is unquestionably the Parthenon, home of Pheidias' celebrated statue of Athena Parthenos. With no separate altar and no dedicated priestess, its main function appears to have been that of a representative monument, a subsidiary temple to Athena as the patron deity of Athens.

The Parthenon has seen its function and fortune change dramatically many times since the days when it was built as the centrepiece of the Periklean building programme. Earthquakes and fires have wreaked their havoc, while Romans, Christians and Muslims have adopted and adapted it for their own purposes. Yet in spite of all the damage it has suffered, it has been admired for centuries. Its harmonious beauty, sophisticated architecture and the extraordinary splendour of its sculptural decoration have been universally praised and the temple considered the crowning cultural achievement of the foremost Greek city state at the apex of her prosperity and political power. As such it has left a lasting impression on the culture of Western Europe.

From the time of its erection the Parthenon had, in fact, been intended as a symbol of the triumph of Greek Classical civilisation. It was built to replace an earlier temple that – while still not completed – had been destroyed when the Persians sacked the Akropolis in 480 BC.

This invasion had been a traumatic event for the Athenian population. With the large Persian army under Xerxes at their doorstep, all of Attica was evacuated. Men went to serve in the army and especially on the warships, and women, children and the elderly were evacuated to the neighbouring islands of Salamis and Aigina and to Troizen in the Peloponnese, taking with them also the ancient olive-wood statue of Athena Polias. From here, they had to watch as their city went up in flames and their lands were destroyed. Of the handful of guardians that had remained on the Akropolis, some threw themselves off the rock while others were slaughtered at the altars, and 'when all lay dead, they [the Persians] pillaged the temple and set all of the Akropolis on fire' (Herodotus, *Histories* 8.53).

As a tangible reminder of the Persians' impiety – but also of their ultimate defeat at the hands of the Athenians – architectural elements of the two main temples that had been destroyed were visibly incorporated into the Akropolis walls and can still be seen when looking up from the Agora today: unfluted column drums from the half-finished older Parthenon, and long stretches of architraves, frieze and cornices of the Old Athena Temple. For a long time the destroyed temples had been retained as ruined memorials in the same way that Coventry Cathedral or the Gedächtniskirche in Berlin are preserved today. An oath sworn before the battle of Plataia – as related by the fourth century BC orator Lykourgos – is supposed to have enshrined this commitment: 'I will not rebuild a single one of the shrines which the barbarians have burnt and razed but will allow them to remain for future generations as a memorial of the barbarians' impiety'.

All this changed, however, when the Athenians under Perikles initiated the ambitious building programme on the Akropolis. The new buildings were both

offerings to the gods in return for the divinely inspired victory over the Persians and a testament to the glory of the now fully formed, confident democratic Athenian state. In the buildings that rose from the ruins, the Greek victory in the Persian wars was now elevated to new heights, particularly in the elaborate sculptural programme that adorned the Parthenon. For this programme, architects, sculptors and workmen would have been drawn together from all over Greece, resulting in a pool of creative talent of previously unknown dimensions. Led by visionary artistic personalities such as Pheidias, they grew together to achieve a common style of the highest order. The extraordinary buzz and excitement in this community would have both fed off and reflected the vibrant public life of Classical Athens, a democracy in which every citizen was called on actively to determine the day-to-day politics of his city, and in which art was not just decorative but served as a forum for reflection and discussion in this social and political process.

The Parthenon was built between 447 and 432 BC by the architects Iktinos and Kallikrates as the centrepiece of the building programme. It was a triumph of architecture, a bold plain structure full of subtle detail. To fifth-century Athenians it would have been known simply as the *naos*, or *neos* – meaning the

The Parthenon (west elevation). The building has been at the heart of a remarkable conservation and restoration programme since 1975, in the process of which many new insights into the temple's history have been gained.

house of the god. The term 'Parthenon' (chamber of the maiden or maidens) was probably applied at first only to the western part, and extended to the whole building no earlier than the fourth century BC.

Marble for the Parthenon, as for the other buildings on the Akropolis, was quarried from the south side of Mount Pentelikon, about seventeen kilometres northeast of the city. The half-finished marble blocks, characterized by a warmth of colour not found in the whiter marbles of islands such as Paros, made their journey to the city on sledges and mule carts, and were hauled into position by huge winches. One of the old mules that had worked on this project, an anecdote reports, was voted board and lodging at public expense for its services. The undertaking was certainly huge: by way of comparison, accounts dealing with the large marble porch on the East façade of the Telesterion at Eleusis, built in the 350s–330s BC, record that it took thirty-three teams of draft animals three days to drag each column drum from the quarry to the sanctuary, covering a distance of thirty-three kilometres (double the distance of Athens to Mount Pentelikon) at a cost of 400 drachmas per drum.

The result was a Parthenon that, with a colonnade of eight by seventeen columns on a three-stepped base of approximately twenty-six by sixty-nine metres, was one of the largest temples on the Greek mainland. Its architecture combined elements of different architectural orders: a surrounding colonnade of plain yet elegant Doric columns, a frieze around the outside of the interior chamber as is typical for the Ionic order, and four graceful Ionic or perhaps early Corinthian columns in the rear part of the chamber. Optical refinements, including the curvature of the platform and steps, the thickening of columns as if pushed down by the weight of the roof, and the tilting of elements high on the building, all attest to an astonishing degree of precision in the construction. Inside, the *cella* consisted of two chambers: the larger, facing east, housed the Athena statue created by Pheidias, surrounded by a two-storey colonnade of Doric columns, while the smaller, facing west, was the treasury, containing vast numbers of dedications and ritual objects that were administered by a board of ten Treasurers. Each chamber was fronted by six smaller columns. A small shrine and circular altar in the north colonnade, traces of which were discovered only recently, must have stood on the spot of an older sanctuary that could not be built over and may have belonged to Athena Ergane.

Like the other buildings on the Akropolis, the Parthenon would have appeared to the ancient visitor not just as a gleaming white marble building, but one highlighted with added colour. For example, mouldings were decorated with floral and linear motifs, triglyphs and guttae (the parts between the blocks of relief called metopes) were painted dark blue, the ceilings had deep blue coffers with gilded stars, and the frieze and metopes probably had dark blue backgrounds with figures enlivened with both paint and additions in gilded bronze. The statue inside would also have deeply impressed the observer with its gleaming dress of gold and flesh of ivory, standing out brightly from the dim interior and lit only through the door and two windows. The nine-metre-high statue was the masterpiece of the sculptor Pheidias and is today known only from greatly inferior and smaller scale Roman copies. Dedicated in 438 BC, some years before the temple was finished, it cost the extraordinary sum of about eight hundred talents (in modern terms perhaps around a hundred million pounds), compared with some five hundred talents required for the whole temple.

The Parthenon's sculptural decoration matches its architectural mastery. It represents the high point of Classical art, further developing the new understanding of the human figure that had begun to emerge over the early decades of the fifth century BC. The body's own forces and energy are represented in an entirely new way that reflects an understanding of mankind's self-determination and responsibility – as the contemporary philosopher Protagoras put it, 'man is the measure of all things'. Yet man is also a part of a complex social network, and thus the sculptures express in stone the same ideals of symmetry, harmony, order, precision and self-control that as ideals also pervaded Classical Athenian society as a whole. It may be the mixture of this newly-found self-confidence, boosted by victory over the Persians, and the realization of the fragility of the human condition that emerged through the dangers and hardship of the war, that makes the sculptures so freshly appealing to generation after generation.

Both pediments featured myths about Athens and present the city as particularly favoured by the gods. In the West, Athena and Poseidon were seen struggling for supremacy over Attica, a contest set at the time of Kekrops, the mythical first king of Athens, when a new race of Athenians emerged. Indigenous Athenians are represented as inherently superior, favoured and protected by the Olympian gods and well worth being competed for. The East showed Athena's birth out of the head of Zeus, thus laying claim to the idea that both the king of the Greek gods and his daughter favoured this blessed city. Both pediments are only partially preserved today, but much of their original composition is indicated in drawings made by Jacques Carrey in 1674, before the explosion of a gunpowder depot inside the Parthenon during the Venetian siege of 1687 caused catastrophic destruction.

The metopes – square blocks of relief sculpture around the building's perimeter above the columns – displayed scenes from four mythical fights: the gods against the giants, the Greeks against Troy, the Athenians against the Amazons, and the Greek Lapiths against the Centaurs (the only sequence to escape defacement by early Christians). It is here that the ideological message of the Parthenon as a victory monument comes out most clearly, for these battles between forces of order and civilization (the Greeks and the gods) and wild, barbarian, uncivilized or Eastern enemies are clearly intended to evoke the Greek

The figure of Iris, the messenger goddess and charioteer of Poseidon, from the Parthenon's West pediment. As she flies, her drapery is pressed flat against her skin. There are cuttings in her shoulders for a pair of wings. About 438–432 BC.

A Greek fights a centaur, an allegory of order and civilization prevailing over wild barbarians, mirroring the Greek victory over the Persians. The composition and workmanship of this metope have always been greatly admired. Parthenon South Metope 27. About 445–438 BC.

victory over a barbarian people from the East: the Persians.

The frieze surrounds the top of the wall of the interior part of the building. Designed as a whole, its individual slabs were finished *in situ*, so that the transitions between the slabs appear seamless. The theme of the frieze is the procession that formed part of the Panathenaic festival, or rather an idealized version thereof, incorporating elements of both procession and games. Beginning in the west, it shows horsemen, charioteers with warriors (the *apobates* competition, where warriors jumped on and off chariots), a sacrificial procession with musicians, animals and cultic implements, city dignitaries, and finally, over the east door, the presentation of the peplos in the presence of the gods (see p.13). Of course, the Panathenaic procession would never have been as beautifully rhythmical as it appears on the frieze; it must have been noisy and messy, following on from competitions that may have seemed like a local football match and talent competition rolled into one. Nevertheless, in this idealized rendering the procession is celebrated as the ultimate moment of civic and democratic unity. By showing all the Olympians in attendance, the frieze also subtly equates the Akropolis with Mount Olympus, the dwelling place of the gods, once more hinting at Athens as the favoured city of the gods.

All in all, the Parthenon presents itself as a splendid celebration of Athenian glory – of unity, democracy, piety, art and culture. But this cultural high point was in part based on empire. By the time the Parthenon was built Athens had for some three decades been head of a league of Greek cities, the Delian League, which had been formed as a defensive union against possible further attacks by the Persians. Centred around the Aegean island of Delos it comprised over time nearly 250 cities. After the battle on the Eurymedon in the 460s BC the Persian threat had much receded, and some time between 463–449 BC a peace was even concluded with Persia. Athens, however, was reluctant to let go of its allies, and gradually transformed the League into an Athenian empire. In 454 BC, the League's treasury was transferred to the Athenian Akropolis, and Athena became its official divine patron. Decision-making and power soon lay with the Athenian assembly, member states were increasingly oppressed and their monetary contributions to the League were controlled and ultimately misappropriated by Athens. This money was crucial to the functioning of Athenian democracy: the state-pay given to soldiers and citizens who fulfilled political public duties was derived in part from allied tribute. Tribute also partly financed the building programme on the Akropolis, which cost a total of about 3,000 talents. A famous anecdote (Plutarch, *Life of Perikles* 12) recounts how Perikles was accused by a political rival of squandering the allies' money on the building programme, 'decking the city out like a prostitute with thousand-talent temples', but to most Athenians, believing in the inherent superiority of Athens, this procedure appears to have been quite acceptable. Internal cohesion, patriotic feelings and even egalitarian ideology were certainly strengthened by turning energies against outsiders and rivals. One might even say that Athenian imperialism was thus closely linked to democracy. The continued stability of Athenian democracy in the fourth century BC, without much external financial back-up, of course makes it clear that exploitation of allies was not a necessary prerequisite for democracy – although it certainly helped the creation of such highly elaborate buildings as the Parthenon, which had no equivalents in fourth-century Athens.

The Erechtheion

In contrast to the massive Parthenon with its spectacular statue and rich sculptural decoration, the Erechtheion, with its slender columns, graceful Ionic capitals and delicate ornamentation, was small and elegant. Yet this was the temple that was at the heart of the cults on the Athenian Akropolis. Its name, Erechtheion, appears only in the Roman period, in the second century AD. To the Classical Athenian, the Erechtheion would simply have been 'the ancient temple' (ancient because of its ancient cult statue) or 'the temple on the Akropolis in which the ancient image stands'. Of all the Akropolis buildings it is certainly the most mysterious – it was home to several ancient cults and it housed the most sacred of Athenian cult statues, that of Athena Polias.

Construction of the Erechtheion began well after Perikles had died in 429 BC, probably not much before 420 BC, although it may have been planned earlier. It was completed in 406–405 BC. By then, Athenians had suffered much during nearly thirty years of war against Sparta and were about to face a final crushing defeat. The fact that the Erechtheion along with other major buildings was still erected at this time speaks of the Athenians' determination as well as their continued financial exploitation of allied states, who were also drawn upon to finance the war. It was standard procedure in Classical Athens for commissions to oversee works and publicly account for the money spent, and we are lucky that the Erechtheion's building accounts, inscribed on stone, have survived. They provide rare information on the economics of Classical temple building and the social structure of the workforce. There we find recorded the names of 110 different workmen, including masons, carpenters, sculptors, painters, labourers, and providers of gold, wood, and lead. Also preserved are details such as the fact that it took five men twenty-two days to flute a column, and that a principle of equality applied to the whole workforce: Athenian citizens (50%), resident aliens (28%) and slaves (22%) worked side by side for equal wages.

The temple that is their combined achievement is a rectangular building fronted by six columns on its short side in the east. A second large porch with six columns adjoins the western end of its north side. A third smaller porch with a roof supported by six statues of maidens, called Caryatids, is attached on the southern side. Finally, a large walled courtyard, enclosing a small shrine, juts out from the building's western end. It would have been by far the most complicated and colourful building on the Akropolis, with rich decorative details, some painted in bright colours, others gilded or enhanced with multicoloured beads of glass. Even the sculpted frieze (its theme remains unclear) that runs around the top of the building displays a unique colour-contrast technique: separately carved high relief marble figures or groups were pegged to a background of dark bluish Eleusinian limestone. An impression of the building in all its colourful splendour can be gained from the modern Athenian Academy (1859–1897, architect Theophil Hansen), for which the Erechtheion's architectural details served as inspiration.

With its highly irregular conglomerate plan the Erechtheion is, in fact, completely unlike most Greek temples. This must be largely the result of both the need to incorporate a good dozen important ancient cults, formerly distinct and now all under one roof, even if in several rooms, porches and courtyards, and to accommodate differences in the terrain. Its complex form would have recalled an ancient palace, quite appropriate for a temple housing among others the shrine of Erechtheus, ancestral king of Athens. Perhaps more than anywhere else the Erechtheion reveals that the Akropolis was not just a sanctuary: it was a landscape of memory, where the past was carefully woven into the fabric of new buildings, revealing and manipulating the history of places and peoples. On the Parthenon, it is through the choice of the myths displayed that the past is related to the present; in the Erechtheion, it is the cults themselves that are the bridge across the centuries.

Exactly how all the cults were arranged inside the Erechtheion is not entirely clear, as the interior was largely destroyed when it was turned successively into a church, a Frankish governor's residence, and finally an Ottoman harem. The ancient cult of Athena Polias must have been the dominant cult: it was in the

Erechtheion that the ancient olive wood cult-statue of the goddess was kept after its old temple had been destroyed by the Persians, next to a famous golden lamp with an eternal flame. In addition, Zeus was worshipped here, along with Erechtheus, mythical first king of Athens, Hephaistos, Boutes, and Poseidon, god of the sea. In the northern porch an opening in the pavement (a corresponding hole was reserved in the ceiling) reveals fissures and indentations in the rock below that were believed to be the marks of Poseidon's trident or of Zeus' thunderbolt. They relate to the contest between Athena and Poseidon for the Attic land (the myth represented on the Parthenon's West pediment) in which each god produced a gift: Athena created an olive tree, Poseidon a salt spring by striking the rock with his trident. Zeus intervened to put an end to the struggle. The olive was judged more useful by the Athenians, and Athena was pronounced the victor.

Just outside, to the west, a precinct once contained the sacred olive tree of Athena, which miraculously sprouted again after having been burnt in the Persian sack of the Akropolis in 480 BC. It was an example to all Athenians, encouraging them to rebuild life in the destroyed city. The olive that stands roughly in this area today reminds us how this temple once would have been the focus of a living community of worshippers.

The part of the building that would have struck the visitor first upon walking up to the temple from the Akropolis gates was the Caryatid porch, with its six female figures supporting the roof. Who are these maidens? They look like sisters of the young women participating in the Panathenaic procession on the Parthenon frieze: undergirt dress, shoulder-pinned back-mantle, elaborate old-fashioned plaited hair, and holding bowls (*phialai*) for pouring liquids as an offering to the gods. Presumably they represent the aristocratic Athenian women who served Athena Polias and the heroes worshipped with her in the Erechtheion, notably Kekrops, whose tomb was believed to have been located underneath the porch. They can thus be seen as successors to the *korai*, the numerous brightly painted Archaic marble statues of maidens that used to be set up in the sixth century BC on the Akropolis by members of the aristocracy. The Caryatids seem to recall them with their traditional hairdo and static pose, and the idea of using female figures as columns stands firmly in an Archaic tradition. But unlike the *korai*, the Classical Caryatids are part of a state-funded building, watched over by a committee of citizens, its workmen equally drawn from the full spread of Athenian population – a single public monument erected for and by the whole of the Athenian people. If indeed this were a monument sponsored by traditional aristocratic forces in Classical Athens, as has been suggested by some scholars, then these, too, operated firmly within a democratic framework.

The Athena Nike temple

Around 425 BC, just before work began on the Erechtheion, the third of the main temples to Athena on the Akropolis was built: that of Athena Nike. Located to the right of the Propylaia, on a spur projecting from the Akropolis on its western side, it is the first sanctuary the visitor sees when approaching the citadel. Long before Athena Nike became guardian of the approach the spur had been a walled bastion. Indeed, remains dating from Mycenaean times are exposed through two niches deliberately left open in the Classical bastion wall below the temple: a 'window into the past' that is another very tangible instance of Classical Athenian awareness of history.

On top of the bastion, the elegant, small Classical temple which replaced an earlier building and housed an ancient cult statue, stood on a three-stepped base with a row of four Ionic columns both at the front and at the back. The temple's entrance faced inwards towards the Akropolis, and an altar was placed to the east of the temple.

As with the Erechtheion, it seems that the Athena Nike temple had originally been planned as a part of the Periklean building programme; the decree issued by the Athenian assembly that commissions Kallikrates to design a new temple, altar and doors dates from the 430s or even the 440s BC. Its execution was somewhat later, however, and like the Erechtheion, the Nike temple was built in the graceful, decorative Ionic order and stands in marked contrast to the sturdier and plainer Doric Parthenon and Propylaia. Indeed, some scholars see the Doric buildings grounded in the ideals of Athenian democracy, while the Ionic temples are suspected to reflect later conservative forces in Athenian politics. In itself, though, the Classical Athena Nike cult was a particularly democratic one. The temple's building decree also established a separate priestess of Athena Nike, who, unlike the priestess of Athena Polias (a married or widowed woman appointed for life from the noble Eteoboutadai clan) was to be chosen by lot from all Athenian women and paid a salary of fifty drachmas a year, plus the legs

The temple of Athena Nike on its high bastion. About 427–423 BC. A small opening is visible in the smooth masonry below the temple. It was created in the fifth century BC to reveal one of the rugged rocks of the ancient, prehistoric bastion behind.

and hides of sacrificial animals. A more likely explanation for the popularity of the Ionic order of this time may be a wish to establish particularly visible links with the Ionian allies of Athens in the increasingly unstable Athenian empire.

Leaving aside political speculation, the main message of the Athena Nike temple is clearly expressed in its rich architectural sculpture: victory. A continuous sculptured frieze around the temple represented battles in the presence of gods: on the north and west, battles between Greeks; on the south, Greeks fighting opponents in oriental dress, probably Persians. This may be a direct allusion to the Battle of Marathon of 490 BC, no longer a veiled mythical reference as on the Parthenon metopes, but an outright historical representation, even though one could say that by the end of the fifth century BC the Battle of Marathon had already achieved near-mythical status. In this context, the assembly of Greek gods centred around Athena on the east frieze, above the temple's entrance, may allude to past and future victories being owed to divine favours.

The victory theme is continued in the rest of the sculptures. The pediments (now mostly lost) represented the battle of the Greeks against the Amazons and that of the gods against the giants. The gilded bronze *akroteria* (sculptures placed on the corners of the roof) were perhaps figures of Nike, the personification of victory. Finally, the bastion itself was surrounded by a low parapet wall (on

the N, S and W sides) decorated with finely carved marble reliefs showing figures of Nike erecting trophies and preparing bulls for sacrifice, watched over by Athena. These sculptures are the quintessential example of the so-called 'rich' or 'wet' style (referring to the tightly-clinging garments) typical of later fifth century art. This beautifully ornate style represented a harmonious world and may well be an artistic reaction to the hardships confronting the Athenians at the time. By 425 BC, Athens was, of course, in the midst of the Peloponnesian War, which eventually ended in Athenian defeat. But defeat was still some way off, and the temple above all was a permanent Athenian war votive, an offering to the city goddess in her guise as bringer of victory, thanking her for her support in the past and entreating her to grant favours in the future.

Nike, goddess of Victory, arranging a trophy made up of captured arms from a vanquished enemy, including a helmet, cuirass, sword, spear, greave, two shields, and pieces of drapery. Chalcedony gem, about 350 BC.

The Akropolis slopes

On the Akropolis plateau Athens honoured its main city gods and heroes. By contrast, the terraces, crags and caves of the upper parts of the Akropolis slopes were home to smaller sanctuaries often of a more personal character.

The sanctuaries on the North slope were mostly concerned with vegetation and fertility. They included several caves sacred to Apollo, Zeus, and, especially, Pan, the god of the countryside, each equipped with rock-cut niches designed for votive reliefs. Pan was more at home in the wild mountainous parts of Greece such as Arcadia, but Athenians began to worship him after the battle of Marathon, which they believed he had helped them win. Nearby was the Klepsydra spring, situated in a small natural cave, with a well house dating to around 460 BC, by which time it was venerated as a shrine of the Nymphs. Farther east, a small open-air sanctuary of Aphrodite and Eros goes back to the fifth century BC, and at the very east end of the Akropolis rock a large cave may have been the home of a shrine for Aglauros, daughter of the mythical king of Athens, Kekrops.

On the South slopes right underneath the approach to the Akropolis and the Nike temple bastion, a sanctuary of Aphrodite Pandemos, Aphrodite of all the people, was located. Parts of the architrave of its small Late Classical/Early Hellenistic temple are preserved, adorned with delicately carved representations of doves, the sacred animal of Aphrodite. Further along the South slope, a large fifth–century BC bronze-casting pit may have been the place where Pheidias cast his monumental statue of Athena Promachos destined for the Akropolis.

Beyond this pit was located one of the most important newcomers among the sanctuaries of Classical Athens: that of Asklepios, the main healing god of Greece. His cult evokes what must have been one of the most painful periods in the history of the city. From his main sanctuary in Epidauros in the Peloponnese, a private individual, Telemachos (possibly an Epidaurian resident in Athens) introduced the deity to Athens in 420–419 BC. The background was clearly the Peloponnesian War with its horrible consequences. The city, overcrowded with the influx of thousands of people from the Attic countryside, soon suffered an outbreak of the plague (430–426 BC), which killed Perikles himself in the autumn of 429 BC.

When they came to the city only a few of them were provided with houses or places of refuge with friends and relatives; most of them took up residence in the vacant places of the city and the sanctuaries and shrines of the heroes, all except the Akropolis and Eleusinion or any other precinct which could be securely closed. And the Pelargikon, as it was called at the foot of the Akropolis, although it was under a curse that forbade its use for residence . . . nevertheless under the pressure of the emergency was completely filled with buildings (Thucydides, *History* 2.17)

Metalworkers in a foundry: two smiths beside a shaft furnace, one of them gripping a lump of metal in his double tongs before the hearth, the other resting on his hammer. Attic black-figure *oinochoe* (wine jug), about 500–475 BC.

In their desperation, the Athenians turned to the gods. The healing hero Amynos had long been worshipped on the west slope of the Areopagos, and statues to Apollo Alexikakos and Herakles Alexikakos – Averters of Evil – were set up in or near the Agora. Yet the old established deities were not enough, so an Athenian sanctuary of Asklepios and a shrine of the healing god Amphiaraos at Oropos in the Attic countryside were founded soon afterwards.

Ancient Athenians would have entered the precinct of Asklepios through an entrance gate (*propylon*) from the *peripatos*, the five metre wide 'ring road' around the Akropolis. The sanctuary consisted of two large halls (*stoas*), a temple, and fountains. To the west of the sanctuary, an Archaic spring, once crowned by a small Doric shrine, right in front of the rock face testifies to the early significance of water at the site, which may well have been the incentive for choosing this place for Asklepios' sanctuary.

A hall immediately to its east consisted of rooms with space for couches, where visitors to Asklepios' shrine may have shared sacred meals and perhaps rested for a healing sleep. The eastern part of the terrace contained a small temple of Asklepios with columns at the front, an altar, and a large Doric hall, or *stoa*, in the north (in Roman times a small hall was added at the south side). This northern hall, set right against the rock, had an upper storey probably with rooms in which visitors were healed by the god while they slept. In front of it has now been re-erected a copy of the original votive set up by the sanctuary's founder, Telemachos, a double-sided relief atop a column inscribed with records of the early years of the shrine's history. At the northern end of the hall a round rock-cut spring chamber, later turned into a chapel, was reached by a short passage. A sacrificial pit on higher ground at the western

Asklepios (seated and with his snake next to him) and Hygieia receive worshippers on a votive relief to Asklepios from the Asklepieion at Athens, about 350 BC.

end received offerings to the gods of the Underworld but may also have been home to Asklepios' sacred snake, the symbol of pharmacies even today.

For those seeking relief from their ailments, the procedure would have been to wash in the sacred spring, offer sacrifices to the god and then retire to a room to sleep. During this nightly incubation the god would have exerted his healing powers, either healing the patient outright or giving instructions on which operations or medications should be applied the following day. The Classical Athenian comic poet Aristophanes describes such a miraculous healing, in his usual irreverent manner, of the character Ploutos, the personification of wealth (*Wealth* 726–738; tr. Sommerstein):

After that he [Asklepios] sat down beside Wealth. First he gently touched his head, then he took a clean napkin and wiped all round his eyes. Next, Panakeia spread a crimson cloth over his head and the whole of his face; then the god clicked his tongue, and two enormous serpents darted out of the temple. [...] They dived under the crimson cloth, making no sound, and licked all around his eyes, or so I suppose; and before you could drink off five pints of wine, mistress, Wealth was standing up, and he could see!

The gifts that were offered to Asklepios in thanks or in hope of healings provide a vivid impression of the wide variety of physical ailments for which people sought a cure. They consist mainly of representations of body parts, such as eyes, heads, torsos, arms, legs, genitalia, jaws and inner organs. Relief representations of medical instruments indicate that not only divine power but also human intervention was relied upon to help cure the sick. By the fifth century BC medicine had become a serious science, particularly under the influence of Hippokrates, the 'father of medicine', whose oath (in a modernised version) is still taken by physicians today. Herbs, therapies such as letting blood, and surgical operations became increasingly sophisticated with time, even though magic and divine intervention always continued to play a role as well. That there was little change after the end of antiquity is indicated by a church dedicated to the Agioi Anargyroi, Holy Doctors, which was erected on the site in the sixth century AD. There is also the present-day shrine in the spring chamber, dedicated to the same saints: in modern as in ancient times, the preservation of health remains a central concern for which divine help is much appreciated.

2

The city celebrates:
Theatre of Dionysos

The theatre of Dionysos, in the shape it is visible today on the South slope of the Akropolis, dates from the 330s BC, the time of the leadership of the statesman and orator Lykourgos. This period, on the threshold of the Hellenistic era, was another time of prosperity for Athens. In 338 BC Thebes and Athens had been defeated at Chaironeia by Philip II of Macedon, a crucial turning point for Greek history. The Greek city states now fell under Macedonian domination and were never to regain their independence, remaining subject to successive Hellenistic monarchs and finally the Roman Empire. At first, however, Athens was granted a short reprieve. The peace settlement with Philip was surprisingly generous and, after his death in 336 BC, his son, Alexander the Great, was occupied far more with his conquests in the East than with the Greek mainland. Under Lykourgos, intent on reviving past Athenian glory, Athens saw numerous buildings splendidly restored or newly erected in a grand programme of civic regeneration: 'He finished the ship sheds and the arsenal and the theatre of Dionysos, which were half done when they came into his hands, and he completed the Panathenaic stadium, and he equipped the gymnasium of the Lykeion' (Plutarch, *Moralia* 852C).

This new theatre of Dionysos had space for 15–17,000 citizens on some sixty-four rows of limestone seats. Athenians would have entered through two gates at the sides or from the top, where the *peripatos*, the Akropolis 'ring road', cut right through the large auditorium carved into the Akropolis rock. Sixty-seven marble thrones in the front row were reserved for priests and dignitaries, the central one for the priest of Dionysos himself. They faced the round *orchestra* (arena) – the first of this shape – with its stone stage building at the back, flanked by wings. This Lykourgan theatre is essentially still visible today, despite later refurbishments, which include the Hellenistic or Roman marble floor in the orchestra, sculpted friezes with scenes from the life of Dionysos dating to the time of the great hellenophile Roman Emperor Hadrian, and Roman installations to facilitate gladiatorial combats and mock sea battles.

The main and original function of the theatre was, however, the staging of plays. In the fifth century BC the tragedies of Aischylos, Sophokles, and Euripides

and the comedies of Aristophanes were performed in a predecessor of the building now visible. From the sixth century BC a simple wooden structure had stood here, right in the middle of the main Athenian sanctuary of Dionysos. Greek theatre had developed from – and always remained part of – the cult of Dionysos, god not only of wine but also of regeneration, temporary frenzy and metamorphosis, in which the performing arts also occupied a central place.

The Archaic tyrant Peisistratos had instituted the festival of the Great Dionysia here, celebrated every March in the Athenian month of Elaphebolion. It included a procession that started at the Academy outside of town and re-enacted the bringing of the cult statue from its original home, the town of Eleutherai on the Attic-Boiotian border. The procession involved not only citizens but also metics and colonists; like the Panathenaia, it was a civic event of major importance. Sacrifices of bulls and offerings of wine and bread were followed by a *komos* (revel) with singing, dancing and drinking. In front of the theatre there are still traces of the old sixth century BC temple of Dionysos with fifth century BC additions and improvements, and of an altar to Dionysos. There

The theatre of Dionysos in its fourth-century BC rounded shape, with later modifications.

Actors from a satyr play, holding masks. Detail of Herakles and Papposilenos, the father of satyrs, taken from the 'Pronomos vase' (colour plate 8), an Attic red-figure volute-*krater* (wine mixing bowl) of about 400 BC. Satyr plays formed part of the Great Dionysia from the late sixth century BC. Like tragedies they usually have a myth as their theme but treat it in a funny and light-hearted way.

are also traces of the later fourth century BC temple, which consisted of a simple chamber with a colonnaded porch at the front and contained the god's gold and ivory cult statue by the great fifth century BC sculptor Alkamenes.

This was the backdrop against which dramatic performances took place over three to four days. The audience would have consisted mostly of male Athenian citizens, but at least by Plato's time there also would have been women, children and slaves – the part of the population that was excluded from more formalized types of political participation. For up to ten hours a day they sat on simple wooden seats set into the natural curve of the hill, watching the action take place on the floor of the orchestra in front of them (still roughly rectangular in those days), facing the low, broad wooden stage building that enclosed it. Rehearsals might have taken place in the building immediately east of it, the Odeion of Perikles. Erected around the mid 440s BC, it was probably built primarily for concerts and musical performances which had just been introduced, or at least reorganized, into the Panathenaia, but it also served as a court and later as a philosophers' school. Only scant remains are visible today of this large square hall in which a forest of up to ninety columns supported a pyramidal roof, either with solid exterior walls or open like a pavilion. Ancient sources suggest that it may have imitated the tent of the Persian king Xerxes, taken as booty after the battle of Plataia in 479 BC; like so much of the Periklean building programme, the Odeion may thus have been a demonstration of Athenian power and victory over the Persians.

In the theatre itself, matters of general civic importance were scheduled before the performances, such as the presentation of honorary wreaths to distinguished citizens, or the release of orphans from state control on reaching maturity. This was also an occasion to celebrate the power of Athens at its heyday: delegates from the cities of the Athenian empire were required to bring tribute to Athens at this time and invited to attend the festival; the tribute was then paraded before the theatre audience.

Proceedings followed a strict order. Performances of dithyrambs by competing choruses of fifty men or youths from each of the ten tribes (*phylai*) would have started off the festivities. These were the traditional bucolic performances at the heart of Dionysiac festivals since the Archaic period, with choruses of young men dressed in goatskins dancing around an altar singing songs (*tragodies*). Yet with the addition of actors acting out the great stories of Greek mythology, these simple contests soon gave rise to the sophisticated plays that are preserved to us from the great Classical playwrights. Their insights into the frailty of the human condition, into the plight of men at the hands of fate, and into the danger of acting against the will of the gods continue to move and inspire audiences to this day. The actors were all men, wearing masks representing the basic types of man, woman, king, slave, old and young. Only in the Hellenistic period did masks become more expressive, in tandem with the emergence of more bourgeois themes that shunned the political actuality inherent in Classical plays. It is these plays that were at the core of the Great Dionysia: tetralogies comprising three tragedies and a satyr play, followed from 487–486 BC (or perhaps later) by a day of performances of five competing comedies. At first all had to be newly produced rather than repeated, so that by the end of the fifth century BC a body of some 2,000 plays had been created.

Tragedies and comedies reflected on the city in all its diversity and social hierarchies, and addressed its most current and burning concerns. Comedies in particular, suspending and subverting norms, were often extremely topical and challenging, airing the views of 'ordinary' Athenians and the politically excluded.

Terracotta figurine of a comic actor from a satyr play: an old satyr holding the infant Dionysos, about 350 BC.

The choregic
monument of
Lysikrates,
334 BC. It once carried
a bronze tripod on
its roof.

The plays of Aristophanes, dating to the time of full popular sovereignty, abound with biting social and political satire and rude jokes about politicians and people in the public eye. Such are the portrayal of the politician Kleon as a self-interested, corrupt and unscrupulous slave to a lazy and irritable Athenian Demos (People) (*Knights*, first performed in 424 BC) or the fantastic story of the occupation of the Akropolis by women tired of war in *Lysistrata*, performed in 411 BC, soon after the crushing defeat of the Athenian navy in Sicily and around the time of an oligarchic coup. By providing a safe forum for comment and discontent, they fulfilled a vital function in the Athenian democracy.

Plays were financed by private individuals, a subtle way of taxing the rich for the benefit of all citizens; similar sponsorship applied to the equipment and upkeep of warships for a year and to the funding of torch races, athletic competitions and festivals. Playwrights who wanted to perform plays put in an application for a chorus and a producer/sponsor (*choregos*), and drew actors by lot. All performances were held as competitions, judged by a jury of ten drawn from the ten Attic tribes. Sponsors of winning productions were allowed to erect victory monuments. For the dithyramb, these usually incorporated the prize, a tripod (a large bronze bowl on three legs), while victory in drama was honoured by money and wreaths with monuments usually in the form of statues or inscribed stone slabs. They were set up either in the precinct of Dionysos itself or along a whole street full of such monuments, called the Street of the Tripods, approximately identical with the modern street of the same name, leading from the precinct of Dionysos to the Agora. The best preserved, still virtually intact, is the monument erected by Lysikrates in 335–334 BC for a victory of the tribe Akamantis in the boys' chorus. It is a small cylindrical building on a high podium which once carried a tripod on its roof. A sculpted frieze shows Dionysos in the company of satyrs and centaurs, as well as the pirates who tried to capture him on a sea journey and who he transformed into dolphins. Of the other choregic monuments only few survive. One is the monument of Thrasyllos of 320 BC, right above the theatre. It has a façade of three piers supporting a frieze of wreaths that once carried the tripod, and faces a natural cave that was later turned into a church. A few years after its erection, the statesman and philosopher Demetrios of Phaleron passed legislation to control the ostentatious display of wealth, which not only put an end to elaborate funerary memorials but also to choregic monuments.

3

The political life of the city: Areopagos and Pnyx

Beyond the Akropolis lay a different world: the lower city of Athens was above all a secular world, where commerce and politics were conducted, where houses and markets were mixed in with lawcourts and assembly places, with exercise grounds and workshops. This city begins right outside the Akropolis gates, where two hills carried two crucial institutions: the lawcourt of the Areopagos, and the assembly place – or 'parliament' – of the Athenians, the Pnyx. One was the Archaic centre of power, not just a lawcourt but once the meeting place of a council with great political powers, while the other soon became the heart of the new system of democracy of the Classical city.

The Areopagos

According to myth, the rocky outcrop directly opposite the Propylaia known as the Areopagos, or hill of Ares, had been the site of the first ever homicide trial – that of the god Ares for killing one of Poseidon's sons. In Classical times it was the location of a council of elders and lawcourt. This was made up of some 200–250 retired magistrates, *archontes* (literally 'rulers'), the nine highest officials of the Athenian state, who joined it for life after serving their one year in office. Of the five courts responsible for trying homicide cases in the established democracy (popular jury courts dealt with other crimes – see pp. 47–48), the Areopagos was the most ancient, important and best respected. It specialized in deliberate homicide (later it also tried crimes of treason and corruption), while the others concentrated on other types of killings. The Prytaneion, for example, rather bizarrely, served as a place for trials against animals, inanimate objects and unknown persons that caused a human death.

The uneven plateau on top of the Areopagos rock is today still reached by ancient, slippery rock-cut steps. Here, the trials were held in the open air in order to avoid 'pollution' from being in the same room as the accused. According to Pausanias (*Description of Greece* 1.28.5) there were two 'unwrought stones on which the accused and accusers stand', which 'are called respectively the Stone of Insult (*hybris*) and the Stone of No Pardon (*Aneideia*)'. Some cuttings and worn surfaces may also indicate the presence of buildings, and only recently cuttings

The democratic procedure of voting in order to settle a dispute in a mythical setting: the Greeks at Troy are placing ballots on a table to decide whether Ajax or Odysseus should receive the arms of the dead Achilles while Athena adjudicates. Attic red-figure drinking cup, about 490–480 BC.

for the foundations of a temple have been identified; a small fifth century BC Ionic temple similar in form to the temple of Athena Nike on the Akropolis. Only citizens associated with the deceased could bring a charge, which immediately resulted in the accused being banned from much of public life. The *c*.250 jurors would listen to speeches by both the accuser and the accused and vote by a simple majority of ballots, without prior discussion. In addition to providing evidence for and against the accused, these speeches also served as an important platform for political and social debate in the Classical city.

Among the countless tragedies this barren rock must have witnessed are the notorious cases of deserters after the battle of Chaironeia in 338 BC and the trial of Demosthenes in 324 BC. Here Phryne, the famous *hetaira* (courtesan) and model for the sculptor Praxiteles, was tried some time after 350 BC and is supposed to have bared her breasts to the jury in the hope of escaping a sentence for impiety. For those convicted and sentenced to death, somewhere beyond the Pnyx hill to the west of the Areopagos and outside the city walls lay the *barathron* where they were thrown into a gorge. Other types of death penalty could be applied depending on the offender's standing. *Apotympanismos* involved being fastened to a board or beaten or cudgelled to death. Poisoning by hemlock was an option offered to the privileged like Sokrates. The latter was, however, also the most expensive method: a single fatal dose in the late fourth century BC cost twelve drachmas. A certain Phokion is reported to have thus been driven to ask his friends to pay for his dose. For those lucky enough to be acquitted, the cave sanctuary of the Furies, below the north-east brow of the hill, was the place to perform grateful sacrifices. This sanctuary was also a place of asylum for murderers and fugitive slaves.

Above everything else, the Classical Areopagos, however, is remarkable for the transition its council went through between the Archaic and Classical periods: it was the curtailment of the political powers which the Areopagos council had held that perhaps most clearly plots the path of the development of Athenian democracy. Elements of egalitarian ideology had been in evidence in Greece since the eighth century BC and had grown stronger in the sixth when first the tyranny of Peisistratos and later the reforms of Kleisthenes (see also p.45) eroded old aristocratic patterns of power. As a result a strong citizen body evolved. But it was only with the dramatic events of the Persian Wars that Athens saw a rapid and fundamental change which in less than one generation led to fully developed democracy becoming an all-pervasive way of life. The common struggle of all classes of society had brought about victory, accelerating the transfer of power to the citizen-body as a whole. As a central part of this process, the statesman Ephialtes in the 460s BC (later succeeded by Perikles as leader of the people) stripped the Areopagos of most of its administrative and constitutional powers. He assigned them instead to the assembly of all Athenian citizens (*ekklesia*), the council (*boule*) of 500, and the lawcourts. All that remained with the Areopagos council was the jurisdiction in cases of homicide, while the real power was now wielded by the Athenian citizen-body.

This major move towards radical democracy – the term democracy was only coined in these years – can still today be grasped from Aischylos' play *Eumenides*, first performed in 458 BC. It puts on stage the myth of the trial of Orestes for the murder of his mother Klytaimnestra, culminating in the foundation by the goddess Athena of the court of the Areopagos. It is a prime example of just how closely linked politics and the arts could be in Classical Athens. Seeing the play staged in the theatre of Dionysos not far from the Areopagos, the Athenian public would have witnessed Athena herself divinely sanctioning the reduced role of the Areopagos.

The Pnyx

The place where the newly empowered assembly of Athenian citizens met was located a little further away from the Akropolis. In the Archaic period the assembly had probably gathered in the Agora, but at least from the fifth century BC onwards the 'Pnyx' (meaning a place that is tightly packed), a large area cut from the rock, was their meeting place.

The hill of the Pnyx and the other hills along the same ridge are now pleasant green and wooded spaces. It is hard to believe that in antiquity these were among the most densely built up areas of ancient Athens. Here, enclosed by the Early Classical city wall, were the ancient quarters of Koile and Melite, two areas that became particularly overpopulated at the time of the Peloponnesian War when people from the countryside sought shelter in the city.

On the Pnyx, in an elevated position above the houses, in sight of the Akropolis and the Agora, and perhaps symbolically above the Areopagos, the great statesmen and orators such as Themistokles, Perikles and Demosthenes would have addressed their fellow citizens, and would have in their turn listened to speeches by less famous Athenians. All Athenian citizens were eligible to participate. They gathered here every ten days or so for half or even a whole day. Assembly days would have meant the city was busier than usual, even though one may suspect that town-dwellers would have outnumbered those from outlying villages for whom long walks into the city might not always have been possible.

At daybreak, thousands would have streamed up the streets to the Pnyx, bringing bread and wine for sustenance. They came to exercise their right to debate and discuss, to decide their fate and that of their city.

These must have been lively gatherings, composed of all levels of Athenian citizens, as Sokrates points out (Xenophon, *Memorabilia* 3.7.6, tr. Marchant): 'Who are they that make you ashamed? The fullers or the cobblers or the builders or the smiths or the farmers or the merchants, or the traffickers in the market-place who think of nothing but buying cheap and selling dear? For these are the people who make up the Assembly'.

What is visible on the Pnyx today probably belongs to the third phase of construction commonly believed to date to the third quarter of the fourth century BC. During that period a large, stepped speaker's platform was cut out of the rock and a massive curved retaining wall was added to support the auditorium, made up of some of the largest building blocks ever quarried in Athens. The Pnyx could now hold some 13,500 citizens. The refurbishment may never have been completed, however, and beddings on top of the ridge suggest that two covered halls (*stoas*) were also planned but never built. Perhaps this change of plan was connected with the move of the assembly later in the fourth century BC to the newly completed theatre of Dionysos on the slopes of the Akropolis.

In the fifth century BC, citizens probably sat or stood directly on the rocky surface of the Pnyx – later there might have been wooden benches – in a much simpler semicircular arena that followed the natural slope of the hill. They faced the speaker's podium to the north so that they looked towards the Akropolis. There was space for some 6,000 citizens. This was presumably sufficient, as of the 40–50,000 citizens over the age of twenty, only a proportion would actually have been able to attend at any one time.

Citizens were divided into four property classes depending on their income, measured by the potential grain yield of their land. These classes determined the kind of military service they performed – not everyone was able to afford a horse

to be a knight (*hippeus*), or the armour to be a hoplite (*zeugites*), and the poorest (*thetes*) would have been rowers in the fleet. The small wealthy class of the *pentakosiomedimnoi* (five-hundred-bushel men) would have supplied military leaders. Yet every citizen over the age of thirty, no matter of which class, was not just part of the assembly, but was liable also to be chosen for one of the numerous executive functions, such as one-year duty on the council, in committees or boards, or as a juror in a court of law. For the mid–fourth century BC, it has been estimated that at any one time one third of citizens would have held a public office of some kind – an extremely high proportion of public participation. And even the poorest citizens could vote and eventually hold high offices of state such as that of the *archon*.

A prime concern of the Athenian democracy was to enable all citizens to attend the assembly – and to reach the quorum of 6,000 votes that was required at least for some decisions such as grants of citizenship. In order to make up for loss of income, an allowance of three obols was given at least from the later fifth century BC onwards. This was the equivalent of the daily payment of a hoplite or a member of the crew of a trireme. In later periods, the allowances also fostered attendance in a citizenship increasingly tired of bothersome and all too frequent meetings; we hear of citizens being hustled towards the Pnyx by a police force of Scythian archers who held cords

Demokratia, the personification of democracy, crowning the seated Demos, the personification of the Athenian people. Document relief recording a law against tyranny decreed by the Assembly in 337/6 BC.

daubed with wet red paint: people marked with red paint forfeited their allowances. As fees were also paid to jurors, councillors and audiences of plays, considerable sums were spent on ensuring the proper functioning of democracy. This expenditure was financed through duties, penalty fees, and silver extracted from the Laureion mines, but also tribute from the fifth century BC Athenian empire, making imperial politics vital for the functioning of Athenian democracy.

On assembly days, citizens entered the Pnyx and collected their token entitling them to payment at the end. The space was ritually purified by the sacrifice of a pig, prayers were offered and a curse was placed upon any speaker attempting to lead the people astray. All kinds of matters to do with the city were discussed and voted upon, from the granting of citizenship to building accounts, from defence to grain supplies. Foreign embassies would have been heard and legislation – prepared by the *boule* (council) – enacted. By virtue of necessity, actual debate took place only among a minority of the audience who made short speeches by stepping onto the speaker's platform. The art of rhetoric was well developed in Classical Athens and speakers would have been closely observed, accompanied by applause, protest, heckling or laughter. This was followed by the vote; unless the case was particularly important, the consensus was determined by a show of hands adjudicated by tellers.

The system of such a large public 'parliament' ensured the wide-ranging participation of citizens in the political process. Nevertheless, there were bound to be problems too, notably in the ability of half- or fully-professional orators and politicians to dominate the assembly. A powerful position was also held by the panel of ten generals (*strategoi*), military leaders of the ten tribes, of which Perikles is the best-known. He was re-elected for fifteen years running from 443 BC and profoundly influenced the fate of his city both through his role as general and as a powerful speaker in the assembly. Plato's disparaging comment (*Republic* 488) about the Athenian people, the Demos, being a huge, slightly deaf old sea-captain, ignorant and overpowered by even more ignorant riff-raff who take over the wheel, illustrates the concern with which the democratic process was viewed by Athenians themselves. Even the physical layout of the Pnyx may have been manipulated for political advantage, if one can believe Plutarch's (*Themistokles* 19) explanation of the reversal of orientation of the auditorium at the end of the fifth century BC: 'the bema in the Pnyx which had stood so to as to look off to sea, was afterward turned by the Thirty Tyrants so as to look inland, because they thought that rule of the sea fostered democracy, whereas farmers were less likely to be bothered by oligarchy [rule of the few]'.

Finally, whenever discussing Athenian democracy, it must be remembered that of the 300–400,000 total population of Classical Athens only some 40–50,000 free male adults with full Athenian citizenship would have been allowed to participate in the political process. By far the majority were excluded: women, slaves (50–100,000) and metics (20–50,000). Metics were Greeks or foreigners who were not citizens of Athens but who lived there permanently and were subject to a yearly poll tax. Even though, in economic terms, the city depended heavily on them, the strict citizenship rules, which after Perikles required both parents to be citizens, meant they were deprived of political rights.

Athenian democracy may have been flawed in many ways, both from an ancient and a modern perspective. Nevertheless, the intensity of participation in communal life it allowed remains unparalleled in world history. It fostered a collective pride and open debate that was vital for the flourishing of all the arts in the Classical city. Both its survival over many centuries and its lasting effect on modern democracies are testimony to its ultimate success.

4

The heart of civic and commercial Athens: the Agora

The Agora as market place

Classical Athens, as a major commercial centre and head of the Athenian empire, was an extremely cosmopolitan place, populated not just by Athenian citizens but by resident foreigners and slaves from all corners of the Mediterranean world. The place where all met would have been in the melting pot that was the Agora, the civic and commercial heart of the city, and home to shops, small workshops, offices, meeting halls, lawcourts, and sanctuaries. Perhaps nobody captures better just what kind of a confused jumble the Agora could be than the mid-fourth century BC comic poet Euboulos in his *Olbia* (fr. 74): 'In the one place everything is for sale in Athens: figs, bailiffs, grapes, turnips, pears, apples, witnesses, roses, medlars, savoury puddings, honeycombs, chickpeas, lawsuits, milk, curds, myrtle, allotment machines, hyacinths, lambs, waterclocks, laws and indictments.'

The modern visitor confronted with ruins of various epochs is left to draw on his imagination to visualize what life was like in the Agora. In Classical times, the open space in the centre would have been crossed by three roads (one of them the Panathenaic way leading up to the Akropolis) and used for competitions and theatre performances; the Athenian cavalry also probably trained and inspected its horses here. One of its main purposes, however, was that of trading foods and other commodities. The shopper could buy wool, cloth, leather and shoes, as well as book scrolls, animals such as pets or horses, perfume, flowers and wreaths ready for festivals and ceremonies. Offerings, such as small figurines or pottery

Athenian tetradrachm, a silver coin worth four drachmas, with the head of Athena wearing a crested helmet decorated with olive-leaves on the obverse, and an owl with olive-spray and crescent moon on the reverse, mid-fifth century BC.

(although pottery could also be obtained directly in the potters' quarter), could be purchased for dedication in the many sanctuaries in the vicinity. Stallholders would have sold their wares from simple tables, booths or carts of wood or wickerwork. They enjoyed a reputation for being uncivil and greedy, and especially prone to cheat unsuspecting folk from the countryside. Particular types of goods would have been sold in certain areas of the market, which also served as gathering places. The perfume-sellers' corner, for example, was a fashionable place for the young and beautiful to meet – in fact, hanging out in the Agora or even in workshops nearby seems to have been a favourite pastime for many Classical Athenian idlers, even for Sokrates.

Fish, birds, olives and olive oil, figs and wine, flour, bread, cheese, garlic and onions, vegetables and honey formed the staples of the Greek diet. For all this, too, the Agora was the place to go; even chefs could be hired here. The lively trade across the Mediterranean provided goods from all over Greece, such as the much-appreciated Thasian, Rhodian, Mendean and Samian wines, along with exotic foods from far-flung regions. As Attica did not have sufficient farming capacity, some staples had to be imported as well, such as grain from the Black Sea region and Sicily.

View of the Agora from the Akropolis. The Hephaisteion stands out, nearly intact, on a low hill above the Agora. Of the other buildings little but foundations remain.

Perhaps the most problematic to modern eyes of all goods on sale in the Agora would have been the slaves. Men and women from Macedonia, Thessaly, Thrace, Scythia, Phrygia, Caria, Paphlagonia, Illyria or Syria all found their way here through specialist slave-traders, having fallen victim to war, piracy, kidnapping, parental greed or poverty. Slavery was common in ancient Greece, but in Athens, numbers of slaves had substantially increased during the fifth century BC Athenian empire, so that at around 50–100,000 they made up some 15–35% of the overall population. Much of the Athenian economy and public life depended on them, for slaves allowed citizens enough leisure and income to fulfil their public duties in the democratic state.

Slaves were protected by law, but their rights were far fewer than those of citizens. They worked as manual labourers in workshops, in agriculture, on building projects or in the mines at Laureion. Every household that could afford it (perhaps one in four) would have employed slaves as cooks, maids or teachers; female slaves also worked as flute girls or entertainers for men during their drinking parties (*symposia*) or as prostitutes. Slaves were even employed by the state, most notably in a public police force that consisted of 300 Scythian archers. The situation of slaves would have varied widely: slaves in the mines suffered atrocious conditions, whereas women from Thrace were highly prized as nurses and grave inscriptions indicate that they could become valued and much-loved members of the household. When slaves succeeded in buying their freedom (a rare occurrence), they usually became metics. Rags-to-riches stories of slaves rising to wealth and being granted citizenship are few and far between. The plays of Euripides in particular reveal that the justice of the institution of slavery was not left unquestioned in Classical Athens, even if it was ultimately supported by its greatest thinkers Plato and Aristotle, himself a metic.

The Classical Agora would have been a colourful and lively place, where metics, slaves and citizens mingled freely. Respectable Athenian housewives would not normally have been seen here and it was up to men and slaves to do the shopping. Female slaves, however, would have frequented the market, and also a fair number of the stallholders would have been women, selling ribbons, garlands, and vegetables. Aristophanes in his *Wasps* puts on stage a highly vociferous female bread-seller, and even claims that Euripides' mother was a greengrocer.

Disputes would doubtlessly have been commonplace in the Agora, but this did not mean that there was no regulation of market activities. The markets in the Agora and the Piraeus were both supervised by officials, ten *agoranomoi*, ten *metronomoi*, and ten (later thirty-five) *sitophylakes*; respectively they oversaw the market in general, weights and measures, and the sale of grain, flour, and bread. In the Tholos (see p. 46) a bureau of standards was located which held an official set of weights and measures, inscribed with the words 'Demosion Athenaion' ('official property of the Athenians'): they are now on display in the Agora Museum. Transactions would have been completed as today with coins, adorned with the head of the patron goddess Athena and her sacred animal, the owl. From

A cobbler's workshop
on the votive relief
dedicated by the
cobbler Dionysios
to the Hero
Kallistephanos, about
375–350 BC.

the sixth century BC and through most of the Classical period, there was only silver coinage; gold coins were minted once as an emergency issue in 406 BC, when silver resources had nearly run out. Bronze coins were introduced at Athens in the middle of the fourth century BC, and their mint has been excavated in the southeast corner of the Agora.

The production of goods would also have taken place in and around the Agora. Sculptors, marble workers, iron and bronze workers, bone workers, potters and terracotta figurine makers had their workshops here. One of the most exciting discoveries in the Agora excavations was the house of Simon, the fifth century BC cobbler, just off the Agora (right next to one of the square's boundary stones), identified by the many bone eyelets and studs he left behind. It was in this simple house that Sokrates conversed with pupils who did not go to the Agora. In spite of Classical texts emphasising the low social position of craftsmen (while praising the virtues of the land-owning farmer) the lines of demarcation were much vaguer in reality. Quite a number of craftsmen achieved considerable wealth and status.

Some craftsmen even had their divine patrons located closeby. The Doric marble temple which today still stands largely intact above the Agora was dedicated to Athena and Hephaistos. Work on this, the so-called Hephaisteion, had begun in the middle of the fifth century BC but the cult statues were not dedicated until 416–415 BC. Its sculpted metopes depict nine of the twelve labours of Herakles as well as eight labours of Theseus, the special hero of Classical Athens, whose bones had been 'brought home' by the politician Kimon in 476–475 BC.

The Hephaisteion, temple of Athena and Hephaistos above the Agora. Possibly designed by the Parthenon's architect, Iktinos, it was built in the second half of the fifth century BC and contained cult statues of Hephaistos and Athena by Alkamenes.

Theseus was credited with having united the villages of Attica into one city-state of democratic constitution and with having founded the all-Athenian festival of the Panathenaia. The main festival associated with the Hephaisteion was the Chalkeia, in which bronze workers (*chalkos* being the Greek word for copper and bronze), many of them probably metics, honoured their patron god Hephaistos, and other craftsmen performed sacrifices for Athena Ergane, patroness of both male and female crafts, such as pottery and weaving.

The Agora as political centre

But the Agora was more than just a busy market place, it was also the heart of the young Athenian democracy, containing most of the offices of its political and legal institutions, as well as democratic monuments such as the statues of the 'tyrannicides' Aristogeiton and Harmodios. They were honoured as democratic heroes for attempting to kill Hippias, son of Peisistratos and tyrant of Athens, in the late sixth century BC. Their statues are rare examples of a public honouring of historical figures in Classical Athens. Before the Classical period, the space had probably been the location of competitions in the Panathenaic games which Peisistratos reorganized; in the 530–520s BC a small fountain house was erected to the south and the important Altar of the Twelve Gods, which served as the central milestone of the city, was established in the northwestern corner. At that time, political life still seems to have been concentrated in another part of the city, presumably the area below the shrine of Aglauros on the East side of the Akropolis. The Classical Agora as the focus of the democratic city was established only during the first years of democracy, when its formal boundaries as a public, but also sacred, space were laid out. But it is only after 479 BC that the Agora saw a real burst of activity, with the building of the Stoa Poikile, the Tholos and the Stoa of the Herms and the planting of trees under the leadership of the politician Kimon.

Today little more than the foundations survive of most of the buildings and monuments that were once so vital to the life of Classical Athens. On the west side of the Agora, below the Hephaisteion and in front of the Bouleuterion and Metroon, one can still find the base of a monument that perhaps best illustrates how the democratic city developed: the monument of the Eponymous Heroes. It was built in the third quarter of the fourth century BC replacing an earlier monument. A long base surrounded by marble pillars with wooden cross-bars once carried tripods interspersed with statues of the ten mythical heroes of the ten tribes of Attica. Members of each tribe could find notices displayed on the base beneath their hero, such as military call-ups, legislation going before the assembly, public honours and forthcoming lawsuits.

The ten tribes (*phylai*) had been the key element in the democratic reforms introduced by the politician Kleisthenes in 508–507 BC. Following a period of civil unrest after the end of tyranny in 510 BC, Kleisthenes had come to power through popular support. The new tribes were constructed to channel and struc-ture political participation in a new way. Each was made up of three groups (thirds) and each third was made up of demes (towns and villages) from coastal, inland and city areas; overall there were some 139 such demes in Attica, to which citizens belonged by hereditary right and which were fundamental to their polit-ical rights and duties. Not only did this reshaping forge unity between city and countryside, but more importantly it succeeded in radically diminishing the power of aristocratic families by breaking up their rural base of influence. The new system was all-pervasive in Athenian life: each tribe selected fifty councillors for the *boule* (council); the influential ten *strategoi* (generals), from 501–500 BC elected by the people as a whole, were military leaders of the tribes; soldiers fought in the army in tribal contingents; and there were communal tribal sacrifices.

The other momentous procedure believed to have been introduced by Kleis-thenes was ostracism. It made it possible, once a year, to send into exile a person perceived to have become too powerful. Once a year citizens gathered in the Agora to decide whether there was such a person. If so, they met again two months later and voted with potsherds on which the name of the person whom

Two *ostraka* (sherds) from the Agora with the scratched names of Kimon, son of Miltiades, and Themistokles of Phrearrhio. Having seen his main rival Themistokles ostracised in 470 BC, Kimon himself some ten years later was sent into exile, having been accused of being anti-democratic and too friendly with Sparta.

they considered a threat had been scratched. The man with the most votes was sent into exile for ten years. Some nine ostracisms are securely dated and another seven are attested. Ostracism appears to have fallen out of use late in the fifth century BC, having in reality largely been used by politicians campaigning to dispose of a rival. Of the 11,000 *ostraka* (sherds) found in excavations to date, many record the names of well known Athenians, such as Themistokles, who was ostracized in 470, or Kimon, ostracized in 461 BC.

Around the perimeter of the open space of the Agora nestled buildings that were home to the vital institutions of Athenian democracy. To the west were the Bouleuterion, home to the *boule*, and the Tholos. The *boule*, or council, of five-hundred citizens was selected yearly by lot from the demes of Attica in proportion to their population (before the 460s BC they had been elected). Though in practice slightly skewed in favour of aristocrats, rich, determined politicians, and lobbyists, the lot overall did ensure a broad spectrum of participation in this important institution, which was responsible for setting the agenda for the assembly, preparing motions and controlling finances (such as the building programme on the Akropolis) and civil servants. At the end of the fifth century BC its office, the Bouleuterion, a building with a theatre-like layout, was erected. Before that time, the council presumably met in the large square building in front. It was also home to a cult of the Mother of the Gods and functioned as a repository for the state archives. Later, in the second century BC, she received a new, larger, shrine (Metroon). The dangers of having such vital organs of state in a lively market environment were caricatured by Aristophanes, who reported the councillors abruptly abandoning a meeting to take advantage of the low price of small fry.

Next to the Bouleuterion was located the Tholos (rotunda), the ancient *prytanikon*, a round building erected around 465 BC which was a repository for official weights and measures, a dining hall and headquarters for the fifty members of the council's standing committee chosen in rotation from the tribes. They were fed here at state expense and one third of them was even expected to sleep over in case of emergency. As a symbol of democracy the Tholos was occupied during the rule of the Thirty Tyrants at the end of the fifth century BC. It was here that Sokrates proved his integrity by refusing to participate in their unjust rule, which in the space of eight months had resulted in the death of some 1,500 citizens. On the other side of the Bouleuterion, the small Temple of Apollo Patroos, built around 330 BC, also played a role in state administration; it was here that magistrates were sworn in and citizens registered.

Of particular importance for the political life of Athens were the popular lawcourts in the north-east corner of the Agora, now hidden beneath the Hellenistic Stoa of Attalos. One room in a series of fourth century BC rectangular buildings contained some juror's ballots, while other court equipment was also found nearby. Around 300 BC a single large square courtyard building replaced the earlier structures. The courts, under the guardianship of the archons, had several jury-courts that decided some private cases as well as public cases that might concern impiety, military desertion, bribery, sacrilege, embezzlement, maltreatment of parents or other similar offences. In contrast to the homicide courts, such as the Areopagos with its body of judges appointed for life, the popular courts functioned through the large-scale participation of citizens. Some 6,000 jurors were chosen by lot for court duty over a year, to sit under the presidency of a magistrate on 170–200 possible yearly court days. Laws provided few precise instructions, and much was left up to the jurors' common sense. Juries were large, regularly made up of 201 or 501 jurors and sometimes even more, depending on the importance of the case. As there was no provision for public prosecution, it was always up to individuals to make an accusation, giving rise to the much-despised semi-professional accuser, or 'sycophant'.

At the trial, both the accuser and the accused spoke for themselves, although for those who could afford it professional speech-writers often prepared speeches of which a fair number have come down to us. Friends and family might help out, and witnesses could be called. For those of a cautious and superstitious nature, there was also the option of calling down a curse. Lead curse tablets, deposited in tombs and other locations connected with the 'underworld', record many such judicial curses, intended to bind the 'tongue, soul, eyes, mouth, words, hands and feet' of one's adversaries. The maximum time for a case was a day, and the length of speeches was limited by means of a waterclock (*klepsydra*), a jar from which water ran into another jar. This precise method of measuring time was, of course, useful only for short periods of time. In daily life, the length of a shadow was a popular if reasonably inaccurate method for judging the time of day; more precise sundials had been known since the sixth century BC but were not widely used. One basic problem was that the length of the hour (there were twelve hours each of daylight and darkness) changed with the seasons. Only in the late fourth century BC was a large public stone waterclock built in the south-west corner of the Agora.

Once the speeches had been made in court, no deliberations were held. Jurors immediately proceeded to deposit ballots into an urn, or – from the fourth

Marble portrait statuette of Sokrates of the second century BC, based on an original of the later fourth century BC. Sokrates is shown as an unattractive intellectual, whose unimpressive appearance hides a piercing intellect.

century BC – two ballots into two urns, one for guilty the other one for innocent. A number of such ballots, inscribed 'public vote', have been found in the Agora. A second ballot might be taken to determine the punishment, which could consist of death or exile, disenfranchisement, or, most frequently, fines. Imprisonment was usually just a temporary arrangement before the actual punishment was carried out.

This is the sort of trial that would have been undergone by Sokrates in 399 BC. He stood accused of *asebeia*, failing to worship the state gods, introducing new religious practices, and corrupting the Athenian youth. With his unconventional ways, relentless probing style of questioning, and critical views of the ethical relativism propagated by others at the time he must have appeared suspicious to many, particularly at a time when Athenian self-confidence was severely bruised after defeat in the Peloponnesian War and the harsh oligarchic rule of the Thirty subsequently imposed by Sparta. Sokrates certainly proved particularly unlucky in his trial. Not only was he found guilty as charged, but his bold request to be honoured for his services to the city by being fed at public cost in the Prytaneion in place of a punishment meant that the irate jurors opted for the most severe punishment possible, death by execution.

Once the sentence had been passed, Sokrates would have been transferred to prison to await his execution. This prison has been identified by some in an elongated mid-fifth–century BC house just south-west of the Agora, along a path leading off towards the Pnyx. It features several rooms along a corridor, a walled courtyard, and a complex of rooms near the entrance. It is certainly tempting to imagine Sokrates in one of these rooms, discoursing with his friends and refusing out of respect for the laws their pleas to try and escape and save his life, but there is little reason to be confident about this identification. The prison must, however, have been located somewhere around the Agora. If not in this building then it certainly would have been somewhere nearby that Sokrates finally succumbed to the effects of the lethal dose of hemlock.

The fringes of the Agora were the place where Sokrates spent his last moments; much of his life had been spent at its centre, mingling where the Athenians lingered and gossiped, ready to use any opportunity for a dialogue. Poised between the privacy of the home and the exposed space of the assembly, the Agora was certainly the place to do this, being the hub of any kind of semi-public exchange of views and information in the Classical city. The most popular places for this activity were *stoas*, long covered halls fronted by columns which in summer provided cool shade and in winter shelter from the elements. Open to all as public buildings in the true sense of the word, they also visually defined the space of the Agora.

The earliest of them is the Royal Stoa, built around 500 BC as the headquarters for the annual *archon basileus* (royal archon), originally second in command of government but later essentially concerned with religious matters and law. He was the official whom Sokrates would have had to face in a preliminary hearing of his case for *asebeia*. In front of this *stoa* the 'oath stone' on which the archons took their oaths is still preserved. Also, from at least the late fifth century BC there would have been inscribed marble slabs setting out the early-sixth-century BC laws of Solon, later considered one of the seven sages of Greece, who further improved on the first formal body of Athenian law drawn up around 621/0 BC by Drakon.

A little later than the Royal Stoa is the Stoa Poikile, the 'painted stoa', which was situated along the north side of the Agora. It was built under Kimon along with the Stoa of the Herms, and it must be to one of these two halls that the recently discovered foundations in the northern part of the Agora excavations belong. The Stoa Poikile derived its name from the paintings it contained, panel paintings by the best known artists of the day that celebrated Athenian military victories, both mythical and historical. Its main claim to fame is, however, that it provided the name for a whole school of philosophers. Around 300 BC Zeno from Cyprus used this *stoa* as a classroom, giving rise to the name 'Stoics' for his followers. Other *stoas* that framed the Agora are the Stoa of Zeus Eleutherios (Zeus as protector of the freedom of the city), which Sokrates and Diogenes are known to have frequented, and the South Stoa, built around 430–20 BC and containing a number of public dining rooms.

In addition to philosophical teaching and dining, these *stoas* were put to a variety of uses by Athenians, including occasional public proclamations and arbitrations in court cases. The Stoa Poikile is even known to have, at various points, accommodated jugglers and sword-swallowers as well as a fishmonger's stall. The modern visitor to the Agora can still experience the sensation of what it is like to stroll along in the shade of such a hall, albeit without the added entertainment, in the fully reconstructed double-storey Hellenistic Stoa of Attalos on the Agora's East side, now home to the Agora Museum. The largest and most splendid of all the Athenian *stoas*, it was built in the mid–second century BC by King Attalos II of Pergamon and is a prime example of how the Agora, and with it the whole of Athens, changed after the Classical period. Foreign 'sponsorship' by Hellenistic and Roman rulers such as Attalos, striving to be recognized as the legitimate heirs to Athenian greatness, played a large role in this process. The Agora in particular became an arena for such generosity, its increasingly built-up central space eventually losing its function as a market place, which was transferred to the nearby market of Caesar and Augustus in the Roman period.

5

Life in the ancient city

A thens and the Attic countryside covered a space of some 2,500 square km, about the size of Luxemburg, and would have had a population of at least 250,000 people, perhaps even double that. About a third of them, and later about half, actually lived in town, so that at least 100,000 people were crowded into the relatively small space of *c*.2.15 square km, making Classical Athens appear to ancient Athenians as busy, noisy and polluted as modern cities seem to us today.

City wall and gates

The ancient city roughly comprised the area from the Kerameikos in the west down to the Hill of the Nymphs in the south west, across to the Olympieion in the south east, and up nearly towards modern Omonia square in the north, with the Agora and Akropolis near its centre. It was enclosed by a long circuit of six-and-a-half kilometres of massive walls, two-and-a-half metres wide and some seven or eight metres high, that had been erected soon after the Persian Wars. In 480 BC the Persians had wreaked havoc on the Akropolis, and only one year later also sacked the lower city. Few, if any, buildings were left standing and most of the city's fortification (presumably not very substantial) had been destroyed. To avoid being bound by an impending decision of the Greek states to leave walls destroyed by the Persians untouched and thus remain defenceless, the Athenians resolved, under their leader Themistokles, to rebuild the walls as quickly as possible. Whatever material was available from amidst the rubble of the Persian destruction was used, including column drums from the unfinished temple of Zeus Olympios, sculptures and grave monuments. The resulting wall had a stone base on which a mud brick wall was constructed, faced with plaster. Remains are still visible here and there particularly in the Kerameikos excavation area. The wall was rebuilt several times in subsequent centuries. It was probably in the late fifth century BC that a *proteichisma* (low outer stone wall) and a dry moat were added in front of the main wall. Connected to this circuit wall at the Hills of the Nymphs and Muses were the two 'long walls', built before the middle of the fifth century BC to ensure a safe route down to Athens' harbour, Piraeus.

Strategically placed towers and postern gates punctuated the wall, and over a dozen major city gates gave access to the countryside beyond. The ruins of two of these gates can still be seen in the Kerameikos, elaborate constructions with a long interior courtyard flanked by towers that could easily trap approaching enemies. The larger of the two, the Dipylon, 'double gateway', replaced an earlier, similar gate at the end of the fourth century BC. It is one of the largest city gates of Classical antiquity, and from it a road let to the Academy and northwards to Boiotia. Next to it, the Sacred Gate gave on to the Sacred Way (or Eleusinian Way) towards the town of Eleusis with its famous sanctuary of the grain goddess Demeter. Another gate still visible today is the recently discovered Acharnian Gate in the north, to be seen through glass floors underneath the new Greek National Bank building at the corner of modern Sophokleous and Aiolou streets, not far from Omonia Square.

Classical Athens should have looked relatively prosperous, much money having been spent on the large building programme under Perikles. But public splendour contrasted with private modesty: 'The city is totally dry and not well-watered, and badly laid-out because of its antiquity. Many of the houses are shabby, only a few useful. A stranger seeing it would at first refuse to believe that this was the famed city of the Athenians' (Herakleides Kretikos, *Notes on the Greek Cities* 1; third century BC). For most of the Athenian population poverty certainly was a constant companion. Natural resources were relatively scarce in Greece and nothing could be wasted. Every piece of timber would have been removed from an abandoned house to be reused, pottery was repaired with lead clamps when broken, and any metal was always melted down and reused.

Few Athenians could have been called rich, owning an estate worth three to four talents (i.e. 18,000–24,000 drachmas) or more. For a modest man such as Sokrates, an estate worth no more than five-hundred drachmas was enough to get by; still, many of the luxury goods that would have been on sale in the Agora would presumably have been out of reach for the average Athenian resident. We know that in the late fifth century BC a qualified worker earned one drachma a day (i.e. six obols), and a sailor in the Athenian fleet three obols. The state also paid those who took part in the democratic process: three obols a day was paid to those attending the assembly and those serving on a jury. Members of the council received five obols a day in the fourth century BC. As for expenditure, three obols bought one a pigeon, four obols bought 3.5 litres of Attic wine, and salted fish was one obol a piece, the same price as a visit to a brothel in about 300 BC. By comparison, an eel, the most prized fish, or a piglet were expensive at three drachmas each. Wheat might cost five drachmas and barley three drachmas per *medimnos* (fifty-two litres). Manufactured goods were more expensive: one would expect to pay up to twenty drachmas for a good new cloak and four to eight drachmas for a new pair of shoes, seventeen drachmas for a sofa, four drachmas for a table and one drachma for a chair. The written works of the philosopher Anaxagoras might fetch up to one drachma. Slaves, however, might cost 150–200 drachmas or more, and land from 200–300 drachmas per acre.

This also puts into context the prizes at the Panathenaic games – a gold wreath worth 1,000 drachmas plus 500 drachmas in cash might easily make the difference between poverty and being comfortably off. For especially large expenditures, individuals might also resort to borrowing money from the banks located in the Agora, from temples or private individuals. Tension between the rich and the poor (who, after all, held considerable political power in democratic Athens) must have been noticeable, but it was partly alleviated by the system of public sponsorship for certain public duties, such as festivals, whereby the community as a whole benefited from private wealth. A pervasive democratic culture rejecting ostentatious display of wealth would have further enhanced social cohesion, while at the same time adding to the notion of an unimpressive private side of the city.

Streets and houses

Relatively little is visible in Athens now that tells of life in the city beyond the major monuments. But here and there traces of houses, of fountains, of small local shrines, of law courts, schools and exercise grounds survive that evoke for those who look for them the daily life of the common people.

As a city that had grown naturally over the centuries, Classical Athens was a maze of irregular streets following the natural terrain and linking the most important buildings and areas – unlike the Piraeus, Athens' harbour town, which had been planned from scratch in the fifth century BC on a rational, rectangular grid plan. There were few large streets, and Classical Athenians would usually have moved through their city by foot on narrow, unpaved alleyways made hazardous by rocks and rubbish. Some remains of such ordinary residential quarters can still be found in the area between the southern edge of the Agora and the Areopagos and Akropolis, as well as in the hills of western Athens, around the south-west slope of the Akropolis, the Pnyx and the Hill of the Muses, where foundations were partly cut out of the rock. They are visible today from modern Dionissiou Areopagitou Street as it runs along the valley between the Pnyx and the Areopagos.

Most of Athens must have been quite densely built up, with houses taking up virtually any space that was not already occupied by public or sacred precincts. The ordinary dwellings would generally have been of irregular shape, quite small and simple, without a garden, their few rooms distributed over two stories centred around a small courtyard, the focus of domestic activities. This was sometimes partly covered and regularly featured cisterns to collect rainwater and cesspits for collecting refuse. Wooden stairs connected the two stories: living quarters above and work and reception rooms below. Roofs were mostly sloping and tiled, but some houses may also have had simple flat roofs. Rooms were oriented inwards, but houses that also served as workshops often had an outward-facing room that functioned as a shop. Simple but often elegant wooden furniture would have stood on floors of hard earth or, occasionally in special rooms, pebble mosaic floors, surrounded by walls painted most often in red, sometimes

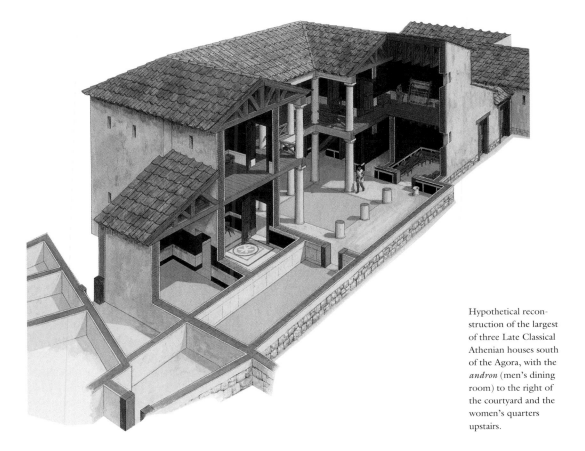

Hypothetical reconstruction of the largest of three Late Classical Athenian houses south of the Agora, with the *andron* (men's dining room) to the right of the courtyard and the women's quarters upstairs.

with white, buff yellow or black details. Lamps burning olive oil provided light and braziers heating. Storage rooms could have large containers (*pithoi*) for supplies of grain and the like inserted into the ground alongside amphorae containing liquid staples such as olive oil or wine. Sanitation would have been minimal. Dedicated bathrooms with equipment such as clay hip baths were rare, nor were there toilets in the modern sense. Aristophanes in his comedies suggests that the courtyard or the street might be used for this purpose, but also chamber pots of various kinds would have been in widespread use, for both children and adults.

In the fourth century BC, a lessening of communal egalitarian ideology allowed again for greater individual expression of private wealth, and some more elaborate houses began to appear. The most impressive and well-preserved of these later 'villas' is located south-west of the Areopagos, in a residential quarter of the deme of Melite, south-west of the Agora towards the Areopagos hill. Irregular in shape and built around a colonnaded courtyard, the 'House of the Greek mosaic' featured in its northwestern corner an *andron* (men's dining room) with a vestibule, both with a floor of pebble mosaic with geometric wheel pattern

Women in a domestic setting: on the day after her wedding, the nymph Alkestis, leaning against her bridal bed in a porch in front of an open door, is attended by other mythical women. Attic red-figure *epinetron* (knee-guard for carding wool), about 425 BC.

designs. Along all four walls of the *andron* a raised platform once would have supported dining couches.

Both these more elaborate and the simpler houses would have been inhabited by members of a family along with any slaves that it owned. Generally speaking, the genders were to some extent kept apart in the Athenian house; the rooms on the ground floor appear to have been more a male domain, and certainly the most elaborate room of the house, the *andron* or men's dining room, was entirely a male preserve not frequented by respectable women. Here, lying on couches decked out with patterned cushions, men from the more affluent levels of society gathered for the *symposion*, the convivial yet highly ritualized drinking party that formed a vital element in social relations in ancient Greece. It was an opportunity to discuss current events, recite poetry and sing, play games and watch entertainment: dance and music, usually provided by girls and, less frequently, boys; girls were also available for more intimate entertainment towards the end of the evening. Food in the Greek house would usually have been quite simple and tasty (if not necessarily to modern taste), making much use of herbs and spices. For special occasions such as *symposia*, a more sumptuous variety of dishes would have been laid on, centred on bread (usually from barley) as the staple and numerous types of fish as the most popular and prized accompaniment. Among other dishes that could be served were various types of greens, cheese, honey, pulses, olives, figs, fruit, cakes and pastries. For the second part of the evening, the actual drinking party, wine was mixed with water (most commonly three parts water to one part wine) in a large mixing bowl, and served out by slave boys into large drinking cups. Unless precious silver vessels were to hand, the pottery used on this occasion was usually fine Athenian painted ware, the rich figurative decoration of which would have provided one more stimulus for conversation around the dining room.

Women's quarters, by contrast, were often located on the upper floor. Here, the wife and other female members of the household would have gone about the business of wool-working (spinning and weaving), an essential contribution to the family's self-sufficiency and fortune, and it is here that children would have been nursed and raised. The house, in fact, was the main sphere of life for the Athenian woman, though poorer women might have spent more time outside: 'So it is seemly for a woman to remain at home and not be out of doors; but for a man to stay inside, instead of devoting himself to outdoor pursuits, is disgraceful' (Xenophon, *Oeconomicus* 7.30). Invariably dependent on a male master, *kyrios* (father, husband, son or other male relative), Athenian women of the better classes were generally restricted in their movements; indeed, wives and daughters of Athenian citizens were subject to strict codes of chastity and marital fidelity, supposed to live in separation from men outside their closest family, although not necessarily in seclusion. Unlike boys who went to school, girls were taught domestic skills (and perhaps a little music or reading) at home, where they remained until they were transferred in marriage to their groom's household. Yet in spite of being legally dependent and politically incapacitated, women nevertheless had their areas of power and influence, playing important roles even in public life through cult and ritual. Moreover, there clearly was a difference between cultural ideal and social practice, as ancient sources mention a number of women with public voices responsible for their own destinies.

The house was thus mostly private space, while public life was played out in sanctuaries, the Agora, the assembly and the theatre. In addition, there were also other public or semi-public spaces dotted around the city where people met on a more informal basis.

Taverns and brothels

For those in need of diversion, Athens offered many delights: 'With its amusements and exhibitions the city seems not to admit of hunger so far as the common people are concerned, for it almost makes them forget food; but for those with money there is nowhere else that offers so much in the way of enjoyment' marvels Herakleides (*Notes on the Greek Cities* 2, tr. Brown), but he also warns of one of these diversions in particular: 'But one must be on guard against the prostitutes for fear of being sweetly ruined unawares' (*ibid* 5). Like any harbour, the port of Piraeus with its transient population was renowned as a red-light district. Within Athens itself, it was the areas around the city gates and the Kerameikos that appear to have had a reputation as the place for 'getting drunk and exchanging unpleasantries with the whores' (Aristophanes, *Knights* 1400.).

Two buildings in the Inner Kerameikos may be physical remains of this twilight zone. Building Y, south of the Sacred Gate, with dining rooms surrounding a courtyard might have been a tavern, while it has been suggested that Building Z nearby was a brothel (see p.57). For the lower classes in particular, drinking (and eating) in local taverns appears to have been a popular pastime; one could simply order 'the barman to mix a chous [six pints] for an obol and to accompany it with the biggest kantharos [drinking cup] he had' (Euboulos, *Pamphilus* 80). Some taverns may have doubled as hostels and some

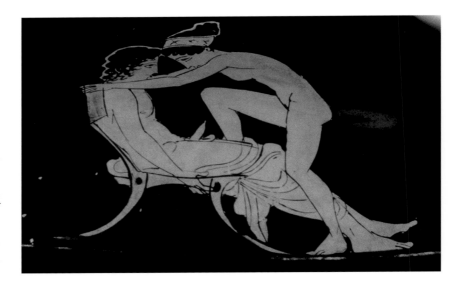

A young couple, probably a prostitute with a customer. The youth is seated in a wooden chair typical of the elegant furniture of Classical Athens. Attic red-figure *oinochoe* (wine jug), about 430 BC.

are associated with prostitution, but in general they appear to have been distinct from both inns (*pandokeia*) for travellers and from brothels. We need to think of them more as neighbourhood shops which sold essentials such as wine, vinegar, and torches, and also served wine and sometimes food. Some may have been nothing more than carts selling wine, while others were well known, established places, such as the 'tavern of the bald man' kept by one Kallias and his wife Thraitta, 'the Thracian'.

One of the more upmarket tavern complexes of Classical Athens has been excavated just beyond the Agora, in the area behind the Stoa of Attalos towards the later Roman market square. One of the rooms in the late fifth-century BC building had a well that was found to have been filled with plates and other dishes, fish-bones, remains of shellfish and shells (oysters, mussels, murex) as well as wine amphora fragments from Attica, Mende, Chios, Corinth, Samos and Lesbos, and drinking cups, cooking pots and portable ovens in numbers that suggest a commercial establishment.

Taverns clearly flourished in Classical Athens, but running them was as looked down upon as frequenting them. Drinking in taverns was chastised by the fourth-century BC orator Isokrates as a sign of the decline of morals, as even the most respectable young men engaged in idle waste of time here (*Antidosis* 286–7, tr. Davidson): 'Some of them chill wine at the Nine Fountains, others drink in taverns, there are some who play dice in the gambling-dens and many who loiter around the place where the flute-girls are trained'.

A similar mixed clientele would also have frequented brothels. A fourth-century BC comedy writer recommends that young men, rather than get involved in appalling adulterous relationships, should make use of prostitutes:

For there are young ladies here at the brothels who are most amenable, ladies you are not banned from looking at as they sun-bathe with bare breasts, stripped for action in semicircular ranks; and from among these ladies you can select whichever one you like: thin, fat, round, tall, short, young, old, middle-aged or past it. (Xenarchos, *Pentathlos* fr. 4 K.-A., tr. Davidson)

One such establishment might be Building Z in the Kerameikos, a large single-storey house with a courtyard and fifteen rooms including a dining room; it was erected around 430 BC and rebuilt several times with the addition of further rooms. Much table-ware, representations of female deities, notably of Aphrodite, and many loom-weights were found here, suggesting to some scholars that this might have been a tavern and brothel, in which the prostitutes occupied themselves with wool-working in slack periods to help make ends meet.

As slaves of the brothel's owner, such workers would have been very much at the low end of the prostitute market, perhaps even below those women who walked the streets. More upmarket were 'flute girls', i.e. entertainers such as dancers, flute players and acrobats who were hired for *symposia*; although often slaves, they could be highly regarded for their performance skills. Top-end *hetairai* (courtesans), mostly metics, often occupied their own premises and commanded high fees for their company.

Fountains, baths and gymnasia

A different yet no less crucial kind of infrastructure for the city was its water supply. An elected 'supervisor of the fountains' oversaw this area. The springs located in the city – notably that by the sanctuary of Asklepios on the Akropolis slopes, the Klepsydra spring south of the Agora, and the Kallirhoe spring in the city's south-east – were clearly not sufficient; they were supplemented by an extensive water supply network built under the tyrant Peisistratos and his sons in

Women at a fountain-house, filling water-jars from lion-head spouts. Attic black-figure *hydria* (water-jar), about 510–500 BC.

the sixth century BC. Water from the hills north-east of the city was brought into town through rock-cut conduits and terracotta pipes, supplying the numerous fountains of the city. One of the best preserved is the one at the Dipylon in the Kerameikos, probably originally built under Themistokles around 478 BC. A square room fronted by three Ionic columns, it has an L-shaped water basin inside from which water flowed onto the floor through several openings. Many houses had their own wells or cisterns for collecting rain water, but for good fresh water public fountains were essential. A trip to the fountain house in the morning was obligatory for slaves and those women not in command of slaves:

I've just come from the well with my pitcher. I could hardly fill it in the dim light of dawn, in the throng and clash and clatter of pots, fighting the elbows of housemaids and branded slaves. (Aristophanes, *Lysistrata* 327–331, tr. Henderson).

Fresh water would also have been required in the athletic training spaces, *palaistrai* and gymnasia, as well as for public baths. Ancient sources mention several bath houses outside the city walls of Classical Athens, such as the baths of Diochares outside the Diochares Gate and the baths of Isthmonikos near the Ilissos river, as well as a bath outside the Dipylon Gate. The latter can still be seen in the Kerameikos excavation area. Erected in the fifth century BC and rebuilt several times, it consists of a circular room with a pebble mosaic around which bath-tubs (probably of terracotta) would once have been arranged in a circle; hot water was supplied by a furnace next to cisterns close-by.

Just as the supply of fresh water was a concern for Classical Athenians, so was the disposal of unwanted water. Of the known drainage channels, the main one was the 'Great Drain' in the Agora, a stone-cut channel built early in the fifth century BC to convey rain water into the Eridanos river at the north end of Agora. Around the end of the fifth century BC branches were constructed draining water from the slopes of the Akropolis, Areopagos and Pnyx. But it was not just rain water that needed to be disposed of: in a city the size of Athens, human and animal waste and its disposal must have been a considerable problem. Private entrepreneurs (*koprologoi*) who removed *kopros* (faeces) from the city were hired to empty private and perhaps also public cesspits, and were monitored by an *astynomos*, a kind of public policeman. Perhaps they made some extra money by selling the contents of cesspits to farmers on the outskirts of the city of Athens. They may well have operated as street-cleaners too, although the removal of human corpses from Athenian streets at least was not among their duties, as we know that this task was carried out by public slaves on behalf of the city-state.

Of all the public spaces of Athens – not counting sancutaries, the Agora and the Kerameikos cemetery – it is the gymnasia that played the largest role in Athenian public life. In the 470s BC the statesman Kimon used his own money to rebuild public buildings and facilities in Athens after the Persian Wars, creating spacious and elegant places of public resort. In addition to planting plane trees in the Agora, he transformed the Academy from a 'waterless and arid spot into a

well-watered grove, which he provided with clear running-tracks and shady walks' (Plutarch, *Life of Kimon* 13.8, tr. Perrin).

The Academy was one of three great gymnasia in ancient Athens, established in the Archaic period as places where young men could take military and athletic exercise. There is also evidence for other, less extensive and less famous training grounds, all typically located in the green suburbs of Athens, where both space and water were available. Ancient Athenians would have reached the Academy, north-west of the city at a distance of some 1.5km from the Dipylon gate, by a broad street lined with trees and – like other roads leading out from the city – tombs. Its course was roughly equivalent to modern Salaminos Street (see chapter six).

The remains of the Academy are today scattered across a modern park and a green square adjacent to its eastern side. The location is confirmed by a sixth-century BC border stone (*horos*). The Academy took its name (Hekademeia) from the sanctuary of a local hero, Hekademos, whose shrine may be a square mudbrick house (foundations visible in the archaeological park) dating from the Geometric period (eighth-seventh century BC). It was excavated alongside an Early Bronze Age house (third millennium BC) which may have stimulated the cult. Other deities were worshipped here, too; torch races in the Panathenaia and other festivals started here from the altar of Prometheus and funeral games in honour of the dead buried in Kerameikos were held here.

The Academy functioned as a training ground for young men, and its main feature was a gymnasium which had fresh water supplied by an aqueduct. It would have been a pleasant shady area, incorporating a sacred olive grove that supplied prize oil for the Panathenaia. Twelve olive trees here were said to be offshoots of Athena's olive tree on the Akropolis that miraculously survived the

Youths in the gymnasium. The youth in the middle is pouring oil from a flask in order to anoint himself, the young men on the left and right are assisted by slaves. Attic red-figure calyx-*krater* (wine bowl), about 510 BC.

Persian sack. Aristophanes in his *Clouds* (1002–1009) contrasts the healthy activity in the idyllic atmosphere of the Academy with the idle chatter of the Agora:

No, down to the Academy you shall go, and under the sacred olive trees you shall crown yourself with white reed and have a race with a decent boy your own age, fragrant with woodbine and carefree content, and the catkins flung by the poplar tree, luxuriating in spring's hour, when the plane tree whispers to the elm. (tr. Henderson)

The architectural traces uncovered in excavations in the area are scarce and difficult to interpret, consisting of an extensive building complex in the southern part of the precinct, close to the modern church of Agios Tryphon, and a square colonnaded courtyard in the modern square between Evklidhou and Tripoleos Streets outside the main park. They must be remains of the gymnasium that became the setting for Plato's Academy. Ancient Greek gymnasia comprised a central courtyard surrounded by colonnades (*palaistra*). Here boys between the ages of twelve and eighteen (when they entered a two year long military training and were thereafter liable for call-up until the age of forty) would have spent all day exercising. This would not have been their first schooling, however: from about the age of seven a boy would have attended lessons, learning reading, writing, arithmetic, and memorising Homer. Classes were held at the private houses of teachers; no state schools existed, but with some 150 pupils at least some of these institutions could be quite large. Families who could afford it also had a private teacher, called *paidagogos*, usually a slave who supervised the child also outside of school hours.

From the age of twelve, when education moved to the gymnasia, physical education began to take precedence, although there still would have been academic lessons in the shady colonnades, as is attested by inscribed schoolboys' slates in the Academy. Physical exercise, done in the nude, was taken in the *palaistra* under the supervision of trainers (*paidotribes*) and included wrestling, boxing, jumping, archery, javelin throwing, discus throwing and running. Physical fitness was of the utmost importance in the Archaic and Classical city, with athletic competitions an essential part of all Athenian festivals. Victory in the panhellenic games of Olympia, Delphi, Isthmia and Nemea was a matter of great pride for the whole of the athlete's home city. Exercise, of course, was also training for war. In the Classical city gymnastic training and competition gradually developed from aristocratic competition and leisure activity to democratic participation. Less wealthy citizens were increasingly given the opportunity to train and, through sponsorship and prize money, even to make a career of athletics, as the establishment of new gymnasia and palaistrai in the Classical period amply demonstrates. In many ways competition at festivals became part of the wider competitive culture of Classical Athens, alongside competition for power in the political arena or success before a law court.

These exercise grounds were also places for older men to meet younger boys, to take them on as their protégés with a strong element of erotic love – an

established practice throughout the Archaic and Classical periods. This is under-lined by the fact that an altar to Eros was set up in front of the entrance to the Academy at the end of the sixth century BC.

Deeply engrained in Athenian social life, gymnasia soon expanded their range of influence even further by developing into centres for lectures, philo-sophical discussions and instruction in a range of subjects, from mathematics and astronomy to zoology, botany, logic and rhetoric. Old-fashioned topics of educa-tion – traditional poetry, music, dancing and martial exercises – were now complemented by the kind of critical and creative thinking that was of prime importance in the civic and political life of Classical Athens.

The Academy was the first gymnasium to become famous in this respect, when Plato founded his philosophical school there in about 388 BC. Many Athenians must have come out here on the road from Athens to listen to Plato expound his ideas, but some at least would also have looked at the great man's ideas with a degree of amusement. The comic playwright Epikrates recounts how he saw a crowd of young men in the gymnasia of the Academy, encouraged by Plato, earnestly trying to define whether a pumpkin is a vegetable, a grass, or a tree: 'On hearing that, a physician from Siciliy could contain himself no longer and snapped his fingers at them for being a pack of lunatics' (fr.10 K.-A.).

Less is known about the other gymnasia of Classical Athens. The Lykeion (Lyceum) must have been located in what is now the heart of modern Athens, in the area around Syntagma Square and the National Gardens, but in Classical times it was just outside the city walls. A road would have led here from the Diochares Gate, at the junction of modern Voulis and Apollonos streets. Origi-nally a grove with a temple dedicated to Apollo Lykeios, the Lykeion was used for gymnastic and military training. It later became famous as the location of the school founded by another great Greek philosopher and pupil of Plato, Aristotle, in 335 BC, with a covered colonnade (*peripatos*) as the centre of teaching and

Boys attending music and writing lessons. Attic red-figure drinking cup signed by the painter Douris, about 480 BC.

discussions. There was also a library, a forerunner of the great library of Alexandria established around 300 BC.

The third major gymnasium, Kynosarges, was situated just outside the city to the south-east, in the deme of Diomeia beyond the Ilissos river. It was presumably associated with the sanctuary of Herakles at Kynosarges and close to an Archaic and Classical cemetery. Its precise location is disputed, and it is unclear whether it is to be identified with Classical and Roman (Hadrianic) buildings unearthed in the area around the church of St. Panteleimon. The gymnasium was used especially by men of mixed citizen and foreign parentage (*metroxenoi*), who after the mid-fifth century BC were no longer recognized as citizens but as *nothoi*, children born from relationships that were not legally recognized. It was thus a less 'upmarket' place than the other two big gymnasia, in spite of the statesman Themistokles' efforts – himself a *nothos* – to 'induce certain well-born youths to go out to Kynosarges and exercise with him' (Plutarch, *Life of Themistokles* 1). Like the other gymnasia, the Kynosarges was home to philosophers, having been chosen in the early fourth century BC as the gathering place of Cynical thinkers. Cynicism had been founded by Diogenes of Sinope, famous for having made a storage jar his home. It was in essence a protest movement against traditional and institutionalized thought, manifesting itself more in unruly talk and behaviour in public places than in orderly discourse in dedicated teaching spaces. It may be that the name 'Cynics' goes back to the connection with the Kynosarges gymnasium, but it may also reflect contemporaries poking fun at these philosophers who tried to live a life of poverty like a dog (*kyon*).

6

At the edge of the city: the Kerameikos

The excavation area of the Kerameikos is today a haven of greenery amidst the busy streets of modern Athens, complete with rare flowers, frogs and tortoises. Here, the ancient river Eridanos still flows, one of three rivers that traversed the ancient city, although by the mid-fifth century BC it was mostly canalised. The name Kerameikos in antiquity referred to the splendid wide street and its adjacent spaces that led from the Agora out to the Academy. It is the central part where the 'Inner Kerameikos' meets the 'Outer Kerameikos' outside the city walls, the home of the deme Kerameis, that is accessible today in the excavation area. Accommodating remains of the city wall and gates, the city's most important cemetery as well as its main potteries, the Kerameikos is representative of the kind of activities that were located at the edge of the Classical city and just beyond its walls.

At the centre of the modern excavation area lie the ruins of two of the gates of the Classical city wall. One is the Sacred Gate, which provided the exit for the river Eridanos that flowed through it in a vaulted channel and paved bed. It gave on to the Sacred Way (or Eleusinian Way) which led to the country town of Eleusis with its famous sanctuary of the grain deity Demeter. The other is the Dipylon ('double gateway') which was the starting point for the Panathenaic procession up to the Akropolis. The Pompeion, the large building between the Dipylon and the Sacred Gate, was where a select group of participants in the procession dined at the close of the Panathenaic festival. A large Classical fountain house (of the late fourth century BC replacing an earlier building) attached to the Dipylon's city-facing wall would have supplied much-needed water both for participants in the festival and travellers and residents of the area.

The potters' quarter

This location, on the margins of the city and with a good water supply, was an ideal place for craftsmen to settle. Although some bronze workshops would have been located here, mostly it was potters that took up residence, close to clay pits that supplied the raw material for their trade. Their connection with the area is old, as already the names Kerameis and Kerameikos have an obvious link to the

A pot-seller or seller of oil or perfume chasing away two dogs causing havoc amidst his wares. Attic black-figure *pelike* (storage jar), about 500 BC.

production of ceramics. Even though potters' workshops have been found else-where in Classical Athens (usually on the edge or outside of the city) and rural Attica, by far the largest concentration was in the Outer Kerameikos area. It was here that potential customers would have come to peruse the wares on offer, or to place a special commission. Pots may have been cheap and their producers hardly belonged to the Athenian elite, but Plato nevertheless tells us that their works were valued by having Sokrates declare: 'If the pot is the work of a good potter, smooth and round and properly fired, like some very beautiful pots I have seen, the two-handled ones that hold six choes – if he were to ask his question about a pot like that, we should have to admit that it was beautiful' (*Hippias Major* 288D, tr. Jowett).

Pottery-making was indeed a well-developed art in Classical Athens, with a highly sophisticated firing technique and superb decoration, and its wide range of shapes found a large market both inside and outside the Greek world. The workshops that produced them would have been fairly small establishments, comprising a few potters working together with a small number of painters: citizens working alongside metics and slaves. Pottery-making was also a dirty business. There were high levels of pollution connected with making and firing pots, and considerable space was required for settling basins and kilns. Both problems were solved on the margins of the city, where space was more freely available than in the densely populated town centre and where pollution and the fire risk posed by the kilns were less of an issue. That 'industrial' pollution was indeed a problem is indicated by Kallimachos' joke about the river Eridanos being so dirty that 'even the cattle would hold aloof' (Strabo 9.1.19), or by a fifth century BC inscription that prohibits the washing of hides in the Ilissos river upstream of the sanctuary of Herakles in the Kynosarges area south-east of the city.

The cemetery

Workshops were not the only establishments banished to the edge of town. Cemeteries, too, were considered polluting, both because of the physical pollution connected with burying the dead and associated rites, and because of the symbolic pollution associated with the idea of death. Thus, cemeteries in ancient Greece were generally located outside city walls, and this was no different in Athens. Most streets leading out of town would have been lined with tombs, in close vicinity to workshops: the tanners in the Kynosarges found themselves next to a large cemetery, while the recent excavations around the Diochares Gate below Mount Lykabettos have revealed bronze foundries next to the large Eastern cemetery. In the Outer Kerameikos the potters' workshops were right next to the largest and most important of all Athenian cemeteries.

A woman attending a tomb. On the steps at the foot of the grave marker oil and perfume vessels have been placed as offerings, including a *lekythos* (oil jar) of the same type as the vase carrying this representation. Attic white-ground *lekythos* (oil jar), about 460–450 BC.

Citizens would have come together in the Agora for commerce and discussion, on the Pnyx for political decisions, and on the Akropolis for major religious celebrations. In the Kerameikos they would have gathered for the burials of their most prominent citizens, making the Kerameikos cemetery one of the main public spaces in Classical Athens. Honouring and commemorating the dead was important in ancient Athens. Funerary ritual was intended to show respect for the dead and, for those able to do so, to display a family's wealth. Still at home, the deceased's body was laid out, anointed, clothed, and bound in waxed cloth. A coin was placed in his mouth for the ferryman, Charon, who was believed to take the soul across the river Styx into the Underworld. Before sunrise, the deceased was accompanied by a procession of relatives, flute players and, sometimes, professional mourners, from the house where he had been laid out to the family burial plot.

In the cemetery, the body was usually buried in a sarcophagus (of marble, stone, or wood) or sometimes cremated, together with offerings, most commonly of small pottery oil flasks, as well as of other vessels, terracotta figurines, jewellery, bronze instruments, or toys. Babies were buried inside recycled amphorae (and, unlike adults, sometimes also within the city walls). Burnt offerings to the dead would have been made close by. The official mourning period was one month, but visits to the grave with prayers, offerings to the deceased and mourning songs would have been made yearly on the birthday of the deceased as well as on the occasion of the Anthesteria festival in February. This kept the memory of the deceased alive.

As the main Athenian cemetery, the Kerameikos contained the tombs of important and wealthy Athenian families and individuals such as Kleisthenes and Perikles, and of those on whom the Athenian state wished to bestow public honours, such as foreign ambassadors. In the Archaic period, tombs used to be crowned by elaborately carved and painted statues and relief slabs, a practice that ceased in the early fifth century BC, quite possibly as a measure to curb elaborate aristocratic display of wealth. Such ostentation was felt to be incompatible with the rise of Athenian democracy; the individual was now subordinate to society as a whole. This is expressed particularly in the simple memorials to the war dead in the form of casualty lists on marble slabs that the Classical Athenian state erected from about 470 BC in the area of the Demosion Sema, the official burial ground for those who had died in battle for Athens. It was located along the road from the Dipylon to the Academy. Recent excavations along this ancient road, at Salaminios Street 35, have uncovered the remains of about 250 men who died in the earlier part of the Peloponnesian War. They had presumably been cremated on the battlefield before being brought back for a burial with all honours in an Athenian state grave. The public funerary rites that accompanied such state burials would have been held just outside the Dipylon, with funerary games including horse and chariot races and torch races from the Academy to the Dipylon, and speeches that praised the virtues of the fallen and encouraged others to fight for the city.

Yet it seems that only around 430 BC did the Athenians once more begin to honour the casualties of the Peloponnesian War and victims of the plague in Athens in a private manner. This prompted a revival of elaborate individual graves. Carved and painted tombstones were erected that showed the deceased with members of their family and often displayed an intense emotional atmosphere and overt suffering. They are, however, not just private images, as the individuals are displayed in idealized roles within Athenian society: the young men as athletes or warriors ready to defend the community, older men as politically active citizens, women engaged in domestic tasks or with young children. Both citizens and resident aliens presented themselves in this way.

The modern visitor today can still relive the experience of wandering through the tomb-lined streets of the Kerameikos, particularly on the so-called 'street of the tombs' that leads out from the Sacred Gate towards the Piraeus.

Here one walks on the fourth century BC street level, below family burial plots on which casts have been set to replace the original sculpted tombstones removed to the museums. One of the most prominent of the grave reliefs that tower above the street here is that of Dexileos, the twenty-year-old son of Lysanias of Thorikos. He was one of five knights killed in the battle of Corinth in 394 BC. His bones would have been buried in an official state grave together with the other fallen of the battle, but his family was able to commemorate him privately here, triumphant on horseback, in the act of killing an adversary. Further along, a typical late-fifth century BC female gravemaker is that of Hegeso, who is shown seated and attended by her maid with a box of jewellery. Just as Dexileos embodies the ideal brave young warrior, she is the epitome of Athenian wife-hood, elegant, composed, virtuous, and in control of the household. With time, as the role of the individual grew again in Athenian society, these private grave monuments became larger and more elaborate, some turning almost into free-standing tomb buildings. In 317 BC, however, an anti-luxury decree under the orders of Demetrios of Phaleron once more put an end to such ostentatious display.

Like the sculptures that adorned the Classical temples on the Akropolis, their present condition is, however, deceptive. The grave markers that are gleaming white today would once have been brightly coloured; usually with a blue background and red, yellow or green details. Some idea of the coloured effect of these tombs can be gleaned from *lekythoi* (oil jars) with polychrome painting on a white background, a special type of vase that potters produced as offerings for tombs in

A grave plot of the late fifth century BC on the 'street of the tombs': the graceful relief of Hegeso, the simple tall monument of Koroibos, and the gravestone of Koroibos' grandson Kleidemos carved with a representation of a tall amphora (*loutrophoros*), a special vessel connected with weddings that marks tombs of those who died unmarried.

Grave relief of the 20-year old Athenian cavalryman Dexileos, killed during the Corinthian War in 394 BC.

the fifth century BC. They often represent tombs being tended by relatives, with wreaths and *lekythoi* left as offerings on the steps of the tomb, and offerings of olive oil being poured from the jars. *Lekythoi* and *loutrophoroi* (tall amphorae used for bridal bath water and offered to those who died before marriage) were also reproduced on a large scale in marble to serve as tomb markers in their own right.

In the Kerameikos the memory of the deceased was perpetuated through monuments, rites and rituals, both public and private. At the intersection between the world of the dead and the world of the living, the Kerameikos cemetery was also the place where divine assistance from the Underworld could be petitioned for, through curse tablets that sought to bind lovers, rivals or adversaries at court. Ghosts, too, were believed to populate the cemetery at night: the souls of those who died violent deaths or who died before their time. Rather than encountering a ghost, however, nightly visitors to the cemetery might have come upon figures from the twilight zone of Athenian society, for whom the Kerameikos was a popular meeting place. At day the place for frequenting busy workshops or offering gifts to the dead, at night the haunt of prostitutes and their customers, the Kerameikos cemetery was thus as much a place for the living as it was for the dead.

7

Beyond the city: the Piraeus and Attica

The ancient Athenians' world did not stop at the city gates. There were homesteads, villages and towns scattered through the Attic countryside. At least half of all Athenian citizens lived here. Together with metics and slaves the citizens of Attica provided the city with its produce and resources. Yet it was the harbour town of Piraeus that was in many ways the most essential extension of the city, home to the Athenian fleet and pre-eminent centre of trade in the eastern Mediterranean.

The Piraeus

During the sailing season, from spring until autumn, trading vessels offloaded and sold their goods in the Piraeus. But the harbour bustled most when the Athenian fleet was about to sail out on a mission:

...the city would fill with the hubbub of soldiers, clamour around the skipper, pay disbursed, emblems of Pallas being gilded, the colonnade reverberating, rations being measured out, wallets, oarloops, buyers of jars, garlic, olives, onions in nets, garlands, anchovies, piper girls, black eyes. And the dockyards would be full of oarspars being planed, thudding dowelpins, oarports being bored, pipes, bo'suns, whistling and tooting (Aristophanes, *Acharnians* 544–54, tr. Henderson).

Before the Classical period the main Athenian harbour had been the shallow and exposed bay of Phaleron. However, when a rich strike of silver was made at the Laureion mines in Attica in 483/2 BC, the Athenians under Themistokles decided to build a fleet of two-hundred warships to be based in the Piraeus. Soon afterwards, these were to prove instrumental in the Greek naval victory against the invading Persians off Salamis. From then onward, the Piraeus played a central role in the fortunes of Classical Athens. It commanded three superb natural harbours: the large and mainly commercial Kantharos (today a busy passenger harbour) and two smaller military harbours on the east side, Zea and Mounychia (modern Mikrolimano or Tourkolimano). By 456 BC the Piraeus was a flourishing fortified town that was directly linked to the city of Athens, some six kilometres inland, by a safe passage between the Long Walls.

A merchant ship and a war ship, possibly a pirate ship preparing to attack. The merchant ship is broad-beamed with sails, the war ship is long and narrow with a ram on its prow, sails and oars rowed at two levels. Attic black-figure drinking cup, about 520–500 BC.

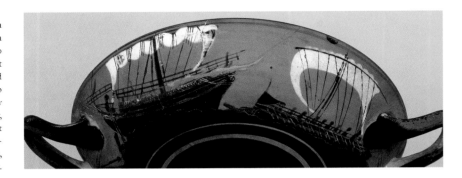

As head of the Delian League that soon turned into an Athenian empire, Athens now continually maintained a military presence in the Aegean and beyond. A part of the fleet was on constant patrol or on training missions, while another was busy collecting allied tribute and protecting commercial supply lines. The fleet was made up mainly of triremes, highly sophisticated, fast and very manoeuvrable warships which were particularly effective at ramming. For each ship, the yearly fitting out, repair and hiring and training of the crew was financed by a wealthy citizen. The crews of 200, mostly oarsmen, were made up of citizens, especially volunteers of the lower classes, as well as metics and slaves, providing employment for at least 20,000 men at any one time.

Athenian pride in its fleet was considerable. When Demosthenes in 355 BC listed the great monuments of fifth century BC Athens, he mentioned not only the Propylaia, the Parthenon, and the *stoas*, but also the ship-sheds in the Piraeus, intended to house triremes outside the sailing season. Some 1000 talents had in fact been spent on ship-sheds and dry docks under Perikles, double the sum required for building the Parthenon. Later, towards the end of the fourth century BC, there were 372 ship-sheds, most of them in Zea, which catered for a fleet of some 400 ships. They formed a circle of individual berths around the harbour with rock-cut slipways, separated by columns supporting a wooden roof; remains are still visible today in basements of modern buildings around Zea harbour. Even the Arsenal (*skeuotheke*), the tackle store for the Athenian navy erected between 347/6–30 BC, attracted praise. With two doors and pitched gables at either end and an interior subdivided by two rows of piers, Pliny compared it to the temple of Artemis at Ephesos, one of the Seven Wonders of the World. Insubstantial remains of this large warehouse have been discovered in excavations at Zea harbour.

Indeed, the whole city of Piraeus was a marvel of Classical architecture. Its explosive growth into a densely populated commercial centre had been facilitated through careful planning by the architect and town planner Hippodamos of Miletos. Around the mid-fifth century BC he laid out the town on a rectangular grid plan. Soon the Piraeus had all the features of a regular city: streets, houses, workshops, an agora, a theatre, and a bath establishment.

At the heart of the city was the commercial harbour, framed by five halls (*stoas*) for storage and trade. Sea-trade was a commercial venture undertaken by merchants who either owned a ship or hired space on a ship. It carried with it the risk of loss at sea or piracy but it flourished nevertheless, and proved lucrative for Athens in many ways. Not only did it enhance Athens' influence over both allies and rivals, but it also provided vital income for the city, as a duty of 2% was levied on all cargo entering or leaving the port. Among the products traded here would have been olives, olive oil, honey, pottery and silver for export. Imports would have included grain (the supply of which was vital for Classical Athens as demand clearly outstripped local supply), timber, slaves, iron, tin and copper as well as, of course, all the foreign luxury goods sold in the Agora. As Perikles proudly pronounced, 'The products of the whole earth flow to us on account of the greatness of our city and we enjoy them just as naturally as we do our own' (Thucydides, *History* 2.38).

The exceptionally cosmopolitan outlook of this busy harbour town comes out most clearly perhaps in its religious life, which is characterized by a high proportion of foreign cults. The earliest attested of these is Thracian Bendis, a hunting goddess related to Greek Artemis, who was officially recognised in 429 BC. She was soon joined by Thrako-Phrygian Sabazios, Zeus Ammon and probably Isis from Egypt, Syrian Aphrodite Ourania (who was worshipped by Cypriots), Baal from Phoenicia, the Asiatic moon-god Men from Lydia/Phrygia, and Zeus Labraundos from Caria. Only with the loss of Athens' independence at the end of the fourth century BC did the Piraeus lose its role as a major trading capital of the Eastern Mediterranean, although its cosmopolitan outlook remained a characteristic feature until the modern day.

Attica

The rest of the Attic countryside and its towns were characterized by a far more isolated and rural attitude. Attica was the preserve of rustic deities such as the grain deity Demeter and the pastoral god Pan, half goat half man. It was a landscape of farms, small villages and towns, connected mostly by simple trails travelled by foot, mule or donkey (rutted roads existed only on the plains, to the marble quarries and the Piraeus). Yet for Classical Athenians, rural Attica was not just a backwater but also the focus for a yearning for the quiet country-life: 'To live in the fields on a small farm, far from the business of the Agora, with your own yoke of oxen, to hear your sheep bleating, and the sound of the newly-pressed wine trickling into the vat, to enjoy a supply of wild birds for the table, and not to wait for the small fish from the Agora that is three days old, over-priced, and has suffered at the merciless hands of the fishmonger' is the wishful thinking of a character in Aristophanes' *Islands* (fr. 402 K.-A.). Peasants were considered serious and hardworking, lusty and vigorous pillars of traditional values that contrasted positively with the supposed corruption of city life, even if they were at times subject to ridicule by sophisticated town-dwellers.

Many Athenian citizens did, in fact, lead this kind of country life and at least half of the classical citizenship was based in rural Attica. Landowning remained

Farmers sowing and ploughing. Attic black-figure drinking-cup, about 560–550 BC.

an important factor in citizenship, and agriculture was the basis of the Athenian economy. Roughly a third of the 240,000 hectares making up ancient Attica was cultivatable and was occupied mostly by small-holdings. Country houses typically featured a large courtyard, a strong tower for living and for storage, animal sheds and a threshing floor. Their fields and gardens would have been filled with wheat and barley, olives and vines, figs, mulberry, fruit trees, almonds, walnuts, and a variety of vegetables such as pumpkin, lettuce, and onions. In addition to perhaps a slave or two, farmers might have owned a few oxen and asses for transport and working the fields, and sheep and goats for milk, cheese, meat, wool and hides. Only few large estates were worked entirely by slaves under the supervision of slave bailiffs or leased to tenant farmers.

Daily life in the countryside followed the rhythm of nature punctuated by religious festivals, many of which are ultimately related to the fertility of the land. Periods of intensive labour (ploughing, sowing, weeding, harvesting, vintages) alternated with lengthy slacker periods, into which many of the longer religious festivals fell. For most farmers their work meant that regular participation in the Athenian assembly was impossible, and also for craftsmen and others who lived in the villages and townships of Attica the physical distance would have made frequent trips to the city difficult, making it inevitable that Athenian politics became somewhat dominated by city-dwellers. The political system of Classical Athens nevertheless made sure to include the Attic country *phylai* (tribes) in the assembly. All of the 139 demes in the territory of Classical Attica, each with its own civic administration, annually sent a number of individuals to serve on the advisory council of 500, the *boule*, which prepared the agenda of the assembly meetings.

The exploitation of natural resources – silver ore and marble – equally shaped the Attic landscape. Mining for silver had taken place in Laureion, in the south of Attica just north of Cape Sounion, from prehistoric times. In the Classical period, the area was a large industrial district, with over 2,000 mine shafts, hundreds of ore washeries and cisterns, and dozens of furnaces, spread over some eighty square kilometres. Its output, mostly turned into coinage, was crucial for Classical Athenian commercial and political power. The mines were state-owned

Olive-gathering in the country. A naked youth seated in a tree shakes down olives, two bearded figures beat the trees with sticks, and a naked youth collects the fallen olives in a basket. Attic black-figure amphora (storage jar), about 520 BC.

and leased out to contractors. Many thousands of slaves (some 10,000 or more per generation) worked here under frightful conditions, digging narrow, deep shafts and galleries with hammers, chisels, picks, shovels and wedges by the light of oil lamps. The plight of those forced to work here is illustrated by the discovery of fettered skeletons of slaves who found their death in the mines.

Marble was quarried at Mount Pentelikon and Hymettos from the sixth century BC. At Mount Pentelikon to the north-east of Athens, the Spelia quarry, which provided the marble for the Akropolis buildings, still preserves ancient chisel marks and half finished objects such as a column drum destined for the temple of Zeus Olympios, or an unfinished seated figure.

More than the mostly elusive traces of agricultural and industrial activity, it is temples and sanctuaries that today form the main attraction for the visitor to the Attic countryside. They are often set in beautiful locations chosen precisely for the special atmosphere inherent in them. The most prominent of these is the

The corn-goddess Demeter (left) and her daughter Persephone (right) send out Triptolemos (centre) to take the gift of corn to mankind. He sits in a winged snake-drawn chariot and holds three stalks of corn. Attic red-figure *skyphos* (deep drinking-cup), about 490–480 BC.

temple of the sea-god Poseidon at Sounion, the southernmost tip of Attica. Situated on top of a rocky headland some 60 m above the sea, the temple with its classic ratio of six by thirteen Doric columns was the first sight for sailors entering the Saronic Gulf from the south. Built around 444 BC it was one of several buildings erected at that time in the Attic countryside, over the ruins of predecessors destroyed by the Persians, echoing the building programme on the Athenian Akropolis.

The most ambitious of these buildings, however, is the Hall of the Mysteries, or Telesterion, in the sanctuary of Demeter at Eleusis, some twenty-one kilometres from Athens on the coast in the far west of Attica. The ancient sanctuary was unusual in that it was home to a mystery cult open only to initiates, with the death penalty facing those who betrayed the secrets. Demeter was supposed to have taught the early Athenians the secret of agriculture and her cult served to ensure the fertility of the land. According to myth, Demeter's daughter Persephone had been abducted by the god of the Underworld, Hades. Having been rescued by her mother she spent half the year above the ground and half below, symbolizing the recurrent cycle of nature. The huge hall built under Perikles with rows of internal columns – not unlike Perikles' Odeion on the Akropolis slopes – and stepped benches along the wall accommodated the thousands of worshippers that took part in nocturnal rites for Demeter.

The sanctuary of Demeter at Eleusis is also a prime example of how religion served to integrate the Attic countryside with the city of Athens. A subsidiary sanctuary of the cult was located within the city, and the festival processions that moved along the Sacred Way to Eleusis started from the Sacred Gate within the Kerameikos area. Many other such links existed between Athens and Attica: for instance, the sanctuary of the hunting goddess Artemis at Brauron, where rites of passage were undergone by girls before marriage, was linked to a subsidiary shrine on the Athenian Akropolis.

Religious integration contributed vitally to the cohesion of the Attic territory. Such unity also mattered for defence. The Attic countryside was vulnerable to enemy attacks, intended to weaken the city by destroying its agricultural base. During the Peloponnesian War at the end of the fifth century BC, yearly raids by Spartans into the Attic countryside (and yearly raids by Athenians in the Peloponnese) were a major factor in war tactics. Many of the border demes of Attica had been fortified by that time, although little is visible of these garrisons today. Remains of a massive fort of the early fourth century BC, however, are still visible at the site of Phyle, on the high mountain range of Parnes that closes the Attic basin off from Boiotia in the north.

The need for such defences had become obvious at least since the time of the Persian invasions, when the city of Athens was ravaged twice. In addition to sea battles, it was the land battles within the territory of Attica that shaped the course of these wars. No site in Attica tells of this more eloquently than the rich plain of Marathon. In 490 BC the Persian army encountered the Athenian army here under general Miltiades with only little help from allies. Miraculously, the 10,000 Athenian soldiers managed to fight back the large Persian contingent, at a loss of 6,400 men compared to a mere 192 Athenian dead. The battle site is still marked today by the large burial mound (tumulus) that contains the cremated bodies of the dead Athenians. A large trophy made up from weapons and other Persian spoils (later replaced by a column probably carrying a figure of Nike, goddess of victory) as well as funerary games at the site kept the memory of the dead alive. Not far from it is the tumulus of the Plataians, who helped Athens in the battle.

The countryside of Attica thus forms an integral part of Classical Athens. In many ways its towns, villages, farms, mines, quarries, sanctuaries, forts and battle sites enabled Athens' phenomenal rise to power. They supplied the economic means for its democratic system, its rich cultural life and artistic achievement, and protected these achievements, and thus vitally contributed to the making of Classical Athens.

Chronological table: the history of Athens in brief

PERIOD	TIME	POLITICAL AND MILITARY EVENTS	CULTURE AND ARTS
Neolithic / Late Stone Age	c.4000–3000 BC	Earliest habitation in Athens	
Mycenaean Period	1550–1050 BC	Ruler palace on Akropolis	'Cyclopean wall'
Dark Age to Geometric Period	1100–700 BC	Submycenaean, Proto-Geometric and Geometric settlements	First temple of Athena Polias? (750–700 BC)
Archaic Period	700–480 BC		
	c.620 BC	Laws of Drakon	
	594/3 BC	Solon archon: reform of Athenian constitution and society	
	566 BC	Re-organisation of the Panathenaia festival: institution of Greater Panathenaia	Sanctuary of Athena Nike established (c.560–50 BC)
	561–510 BC	Rule of Peisistratos and his sons	Statues of maidens erected on Akropolis (korai) c.560–480 BC
	508/7 BC	Democratic reforms under Kleisthenes	Old Temple of Athena (506 BC?)
			Competition for tragedies instituted at the City Dionysia
	499–494 BC	Unsuccessful revolt of Ionian cities against Persian rule	Agora develops into civic and commercial centre
			First theatre of Dionysos (c.500 BC)
	490 BC	Beginning of Persian Wars: First Persian invasion of Greece defeated at Marathon	
	488 BC	First ostracism attested	
	487 BC	Athenian archons (magistrates) chosen by lot	
	483 BC	Discovery of rich silver vein in Laureion; building of fleet under Themistokles	Tragedies by Aischylos 484–46 BC
	480/79 BC	Second Persian invasion of Greece and sack of Athens; defeated after battles at Artemision, Thermopylai, Salamis and Plataiai.	Competition for comedies added to City Dionysia
Classical Period	480–323 BC		
	478/7 BC	Formation of Delian League against Persians	City Walls of Athens and Piraeus built (Themistoklean wall)
	470 BC	Ostracism of Themistokles	Aischylos' *Persians* (472 BC)
	469/8 (or 466/5 BC)	Greeks under Kimon defeat Persians in battle on Eurymedon	Stoa Poikile and Tholos built in Agora (470–460 BC)
	462/1 BC	Democratic reforms under Ephialtes; beginning of radical democracy; ostracism of Kimon and assassination of Ephialtes	Athena Promachos by Pheidias (465/60–55/50 BC)
			Tragedies of Sophokles (468–406 BC)
	454 BC	Transfer of treasure of Delian League to Athens; Delian League transforms into Athenian empire	Historian Thucydides born (before 455 BC)
	460–429 BC	Age of Perikles (strategos 444/3–429 BC)	Long Walls to Piraeus and Phaleron built (460–445 BC)
	450/49 BC	Peace agreement between Athens and Persia (Peace of Kallias)	Akropolis building programme (449 BC)
			Parthenon built (447–32 BC)
	440 BC	Attempted revolt of Samos from Athenian empire	Construction of Propylaia (437/6–432 BC)
			Odeion of Perikles (c.440–30 BC)
	431–404 BC	Peloponnesian War between Athens and Sparta	Tragedies of Euripides (437–407/6 BC)
			Herodotos' *Histories* (finished in the 430s BC)
	430–26 BC	Plague in Athens; death of Perikles (429 BC)	Plato (427–347 BC)
			Temple of Athena Nike built (c.427–23 BC)
			Comedies of Aristophanes (427–388/7 BC)

PERIOD	TIME	POLITICAL AND MILITARY EVENTS	CULTURE AND ARTS
	421–15 BC	Peace of Nikias ends first part of Peloponnesian War. Last securely dated ostracism (417 BC)	
	415–13 BC	Sicilian expedition ending in defeat of Athens	
	411 BC	Oligarchic revolution and re-establishment of democracy	
	405/4 BC	Spartan victory over Athens at Aigospotamoi (405 BC); capitulation of Athens ends Peloponnesian War (March 404 BC)	Erechtheion completed (421–405 BC)
	404–3 BC	Reign of the Thirty Tyrants backed by Sparta, followed by restoration of democracy	Trial and execution of Sokrates (399 BC)
	395–87/6 BC	Corinthian War: Sparta faces a coalition of Corinth, Argos, Thebes, and Athens. Spartan victory with Persian backing and King's Peace	Thucydides' *History of the Peloponnesian War* (396/5 BC) Plato opens Academy (387 BC)
	377 BC	Second Athenian League formed	
	368 BC	Plato founds philosophical school at Academy	
	354 BC	Second Athenian League breaks up	Demosthenes' first public speech
	338–26 BC	Administration of Lykourgos	Panathenaic Stadium built, Theatre of Dionysos and Pnyx rebuilt
	337 BC	Supremacy of Macedonia in Greece after battle of Chaironeia; Alexander the Great succeeds Philip II (336 BC)	Aristotle founds philosophical school at Lykeion (335 BC)
Hellenistic Period	323–31 BC	Death of Alexander the Great 323 BC	
	322 BC	Lamian War against Macedonia ends in Greek defeat; Macedonian occupation of Athens	Death of Aristotle and suicide of Demosthenes
	317–307 BC	Rule of Demetrios of Phaleron	Epicurus the philosopher settles in Athens
	268/7–262 BC	Chremonidean War, Athens against Macedon	
	157–138 BC	Attalos II of Pergamon, benefactor of Athens	
	86 BC	Roman dictator Sulla sacks Athens	
Roman Empire	31 BC–AD 330		
	31 BC	Battle of Actium	
	27 BC	Roman province of Achaea founded under Augustus (27 BC–14 AD), first Roman Emperor	
	AD 117–138	Roman Emperor Hadrian, benefactor of Athens	
	c. AD 150–170		Pausanias visits Athens and writes *Guide to Greece*
	AD 267	Herulians invade Greece and sack Athens	Beulé Gate, Post-Herulian Wall (*c.* AD 270–80)
Byzantine Empire	AD 330–1453		
	AD 381/0	Christianity made state religion by Emperor Theodosius	
	AD 396	Invasion of Greece by Visigoths under Alaric	
	AD 529	Emperor Justinian closes philosophical schools of Athens	
	AD 582/3	Devastation of Athens, probably by Slavs	
	c. AD 600		Parthenon and Erechtheion converted into churches
	AD 1204	Athens falls to Franks; lower city of Athens devastated by Leon Sgrouros from Nauplia	Parthenon becomes Latin Church and Propylaia become ducal palace (AD 1206)
Ottoman Empire	AD 1300–1923		
	AD 1436 and 1447	Cyriacus of Ancona visits Athens	
	AD 1453	Fall of Constantinople to Ottoman Turks	
	AD 1456–8	Capture of Athens by the Turks; Athens part of Ottoman Empire	Parthenon converted into mosque (*c.* AD 1460)
	AD 1687–8	Venetians besiege Akropolis, Turks recover it	Explosion of Parthenon, small mosque built inside ruins
	AD 1821–31	Greek War of Independence	
Modern Hellenic State	AD 1833–62	Otto of Bavaria King of the Hellenes	
	AD 1834	Athens becomes the capital of modern Greece	Akropolis declared an archaeological site

Further reading

R. Barber, Blue Guide, *Athens* (London: A & C Black, 2002)

S. Blundell, *Women in Classical Athens* (Bristol: Bristol Classical Press, 1998)

J.M. Camp, *The Archaeology of Athens* (New Haven & London: Yale University Press, 2001)

J.M. Camp, *The Athenian Agora: Excavations in the Heart of Classical Athens* (London: Thames and Hudson, 1992)

C. Carey, *Democracy in Classical Athens* (Bristol: Bristol Classical Press, 2000)

P. Cartledge, P. Millett and S. von Reden (eds), *Kosmos: Essays in Order, Conflict and Community in Classical Athens* (Cambridge: Cambridge University Press, 1998)

P. Connolly and H. Dodge, *The Ancient City: Life in Classical Athens & Rome* (Oxford: Oxford University Press, 1998)

J. N. Davidson, *Courtesans and Fishcakes: The Consuming Passions of Classical Athens* (London: HarperCollins, 1997)

H.J. Deighton, *A Day in the Life of Ancient Athens* (Bristol: Bristol Classical Press, 1995)

R. Garland, *The Greek Way of Death* (London: Duckworth, 1985)

H.R. Goette, *Athens, Attica, and the Megarid: An Archaeological Guide* (London: Routledge, 2001)

J.M. Hurwit, *The Athenian Acropolis: History, Mythology, and Archaeology from the Neolithic Era to the Present* (Cambridge: Cambridge University Press, 1999)

Joint Association of Classical Teachers, *World of Athens: An Introduction to Classical Athenian Culture* (Cambridge: Cambridge University Press, 1984)

C. Meier, *Athens: A Portrait of the City in its Golden Age* (London: John Murray, 1998)

R. Parker, *Athenian Religion: A History* (Oxford: Clarendon Press, 1996)

J.J. Pollitt, *Art and Experience in Classical Greece* (Cambridge: Cambridge University Press, 1972)

S. von Reden, *Exchange in Ancient Greece* (London: Duckworth, 2003)

J.W. Roberts, *City of Sokrates. An Introduction to Classical Athens* (2nd edn London: Routledge, 1998)

R.E. Wycherley, *The Stones of Athens* (Princeton: Princeton University Press, 1978)

Index

INDEX

79

Picture credits

Map on p.4: Drawing Kate Morton

Colour images:
BM GR 1853.3-7.383; © akg-images/Peter Connolly; Photograph author; BM GR 1920.12-21.1; BM GR 1885.12-13.18 (Vase E 190); BM GR 1873.1-11.11 (Vase E 536); BM GR 1884.2-23.2 (Vase D 59); Naples, Museo Archeologico Nazionale 81673 (H3240); BM GR 1866.4-15.249 (Vase B 606)

Black and white images:
p.9: Museum of Fine Arts, Boston. Francis Bartlett Donation of 1912. 13.169. Photograph © Museum of Fine Arts, Boston; p.10: BM GR 1866.4-15.246 (Vase B 605); p.11: BM GR 1805.7-3.91 (Sculpture 549); p.12: Private Collection. Photograph Dieter Widmer, courtesy of David Cahn; p.13: BM GR 1816.6-10.18; p.15: Photograph author; p.17: BM GR 1816.6-10.96 (Sculpture 304 N); p.18: BM GR 1816.6-10.11 (Sculpture 316); p.21: Photograph © Jeremy Stafford-Deitsch; p.23: © Deutsches Archäologisches Institut, Athens, Neg. no. Akropolis 183; p.24: BM GR 1865.7-12.86 (Gem 601); p.25: BM GR 1846.6-29.45 (Vase B 507); p.26: Athens, NM 1330. © Deutsches Archäologisches Institut, Athens, Neg. no. NM 400; p.29: © Deutsches Archäologisches Institut, Athens, Neg. no. Hege 1906; p.30: Naples, Museo Archeologico Nazionale 81673 (H3240); p.31: BM GR 1842.7-28.751 (Terracotta 736); p.32: Photograph author; p.35: BM GR 1843.11-3.11 (Vase E 69); p.37: BM GR 1853.3-7.465; p.38: Athens, Agora Museum I 6524. © Deutsches Archäologisches Institut, Athens., Neg. no. 2001/710; p.40: Photograph author; p.41: BM CM 1922.11-2.1; p.43: Athens, Agora Museum I 7396. © Deutsches Archäologisches Institut, Athens, Neg. no. 2001/779; p.44: Photograph © Jeremy Stafford-Deitsch; p.46: Athens, Agora Museum P 5958 and P 18555. © Deutsches Archäologisches Institut, Athens, Neg. nos. 2001/721 and 2001/731; p.48: BM GR 1925.11-18.1; p.53: © akg-images/Peter Connolly; p.54: Athens, National Museum 1629. © Deutsches Archäologisches Institut, Athens, Neg. no. 5127; p.56: Berlin, Antikensammlung F 2414. Photograph Museum; p.57: BM GR 1837.6-9.53 (Vase B 334); p.59: Berlin, Antikensammlung F 2180. Photograph Museum; p.61: Berlin, Antikensammlung F 2285. Photograph Museum; p.64: Florence, Museo Archeologico 72 732. Photograph Museum; p.65: BM GR 1884.2-23.1 (Vase D 65); p.67: Photograph author; p.68: Athens, Kerameikos Museum 1130. © Deutsches Archäologisches Institut, Athens, Neg. no. Kerameikos 820; p.70: BM GR 1876.5-8.963 (Vase B 436); p.72: BM GR 1906.12-15.1; p.73: BM GR 1837.6-9.42 (Vase B 226); p.74: BM GR 1873.8-20.375 (Vase E 140)

Book cover:
Athenian drinking party (symposion): men reclining on couches, served by slave boys. Drinking cups and jugs are hanging up on the wall behind. Attic red-figure drinking cup signed by the painter Douris, about 480 BC;
BM GR 1843.11-3.15 (Vase E 49)
The Erechtheion on the Athenian Akropolis; Photo © Jeremy Stafford-Deitsch